THE
BRITANNIA
& OTHER TUBULAR
BRIDGES

THE
BRITANNIA
& OTHER TUBULAR
BRIDGES
and the men who built them

John Rapley

Royalties for the sale of this book have been
assigned to the Institution of Civil Engineers
(Registered Charity No.210252).

TEMPUS

In memory of my father
Frederick Harvey Rapley AMICE MIMechE
(1863-1928)

First published 2003

PUBLISHED IN THE UNITED KINGDOM BY:
Tempus Publishing Ltd
The Mill, Brimscombe Port
Stroud, Gloucestershire GL5 2QG
www.tempus-publishing.com

PUBLISHED IN THE UNITED STATES OF AMERICA BY:
Tempus Publishing Inc.
2 Cumberland Street
Charleston, SC 29401
USA
www.tempuspublishing.com

British Library Cataloguing in Publication Data.
A catalogue record for this book is available from the British Library.

ISBN 0 7524 2753 9

Typesetting and origination by Tempus Publishing.
PRINTED AND BOUND IN GREAT BRITAIN.

Contents

Attributions

Images were provided by the following individuals and organisations:

1. Caernarfon Record Office: pp. 25, 55.
2. Oliver F. Carter via David White: p. 65.
3. Colour-Rail: colour section nos 2-5, 9-11, 28.
4. Coutauld Institute: p.12.
5. Dr R. Firzgerald: colour section nos 6, 29.
6. D.K.Horne: colour section no.7.
7. Ironbridge Gorge Museum: colour section nos 12, 14-21, 25; p.69.
8. John Marshall: p.13, 32.
9. The National Railway Museum: p.52.
10. Royal Engineers Library: pp. 93, 108, 123.
11. Archivist, Royal Society of London: p.87.
12. Dr James S. Shipley: colour section nos 8, 13, 26, 27; p.29.
13. Dr Paul Sibly: p.96.
14. Royal Commission on the Ancient and Historical Monuments of Wales: pp.57, 146.
15. All other photos provided by the Library of the Institution of Civil Engineers.

Preface

The origins of this book lie in an introductory essay contributed to the catalogue of an exhibition arranged at the instance of the archives committee of the Institution of Civil Engineers to mark the 150th anniversary of the opening of the Britannia Bridge in March 1850. Encouraging comments from several professional engineers suggested that there might be a wider readership for an improved and expanded version.

This is not only the story of a successful working partnership between two great men, each supreme in his own field, but also records the parts played by many others without whose efforts the successful completion of the tubular bridges might have been in jeopardy. While it may be that no man is indispensable, there were some without whom success would have been very difficult, and they are all worthy of being placed on record.

This book is concerned only with those bridges where the tube acted as a self-supporting girder beam. Other great bridges, such as those over the Tamar and the Wye by Brunel, and the Forth Bridge of Fowler and Baker, have massive tubular compression members for which purpose the tubular form is highly effective. In 1845 the train-sized tubular beam was a novel concept but by 1860 it was dead – with the exception of Fairbairn's box girders, which lingered for a few years longer.

While the Conwy and Britannia tubular beams offered a practical solution to a pressing problem, in retrospect they proved to be a desperate remedy for a desperate situation. Within ten years of their conception it was becoming abundantly clear that the train-sized tubular girder was clumsy and inefficient and represented a blind alley in girder development. However, the many lessons learnt were to prove invaluable to, for example, the understanding of the behaviour of thin walled tubes, or the application of large-scale project management and, as at Conwy, the employment of a general contractor handling all aspects of the project through to completion. In addition, new technology was introduced in the form of power riveting machines and a programmable hole-punching machine, as well as pioneering the application of hydraulic power to lift safely great weights to great heights. Even more important was the introduction of a material, wrought iron, previously unknown in large-scale structural work but destined to become a structural material of primary importance.

The tubular bridges cannot be considered in isolation. The story of the application of iron and steel to railway and other bridges did not start in 1845 nor is its end yet in sight. The tubular bridges must be set in their historical context. Prior to 1845 iron railway bridges were few and of limited span, yet it was only forty-five years later that the all-steel Forth Bridge was opened, bringing to an end an era of unprecedented development. An opportunity has been taken to explore some of the interesting byways of bridge history so that the tubular bridges can be viewed in a broader context.

Discussion of the somewhat unseemly dispute between Fairbairn and Stephenson forms an essential part of the story, for over the past century and a half attitudes have become entrenched. Even in 1850, after the publication of Edwin Clark's book, which overshadowed Fairbairn's earlier and more modest effort, views became polarised, although more knowledgeable commentators were prepared to award credit where credit was due. Unfortunately, many writers since have accepted Clark's work as a definitive history, ignoring the fact that it was written on Stephenson's instructions and under his direction as a work of propaganda. On this occasion a wide range of sources, which are detailed in the bibliography, have been studied in an attempt to produce a fair and balanced record based on hard facts and not wild assertions.

In acknowledging the generous assistance received from many people and institutions while researching this book, I must firstly express my gratitude to the Institution of Civil Engineers, their Head Librarian, Mr Michael Chrimes, and his staff, not least their archivist, Mrs Carol Morgan, who has borne the brunt of my enquiries with ever cheerful fortitude.

There is little virtue in reinventing the wheel when it has already been done so well, and I am deeply indebted to Mr Peter E. Baughan, whose definitive history of the Chester & Holyhead Railway is a model of its kind, and a never failing source of historical background.

To all the others who have assisted with information and photographs I would take this opportunity of expressing my sincere appreciation of their generous help: the archivists at Bangor, Caernarfon, and Llangefni Record Offices; Ed Bartholomew of the National Railway Museum, York; Dr B.M.J. Barton, Grantham; Peter Billson, Derby; Conwy County Borough Library, Conwy; Dr Ron Fitzgerald, Halifax; Roger Harris, Shaftesbury; David Hopkins, Ironbridge Gorge Museum Library; Rev. Dr Richard L. Hills, Mottram; Brian Lewis; Surbiton; John Marshall, Bewdley; John Millar of Heap & Partners, Hoylake; Robert W. Passfield, Québec, Canada; Dr R.T. Smith of the Newcomen Society, London; Professor Roland A. Paxton MBE, Edinburgh; Sherryl Healey, Railway Studies Library, Newton Abbott; Dr Robert W. Rennison, Newcastle upon Tyne; the Royal Engineers Library, Chatham; the Archivist of the Royal Society of London; Dr James S. Shipway, Edinburgh; Dr Paul Sibly, Nottingham; Donald A. Steggles, Exeter; R.J.M. Sutherland, London; the Archivist, UMIST, Manchester; University College Library, London; David M.B. White, Carmarthen. My sincere apologies to any whom I have inadvertently omitted.

I must, however, express my special thanks to Mr D.K. Horne of Ross on Wye who has placed a lifetime's experience of structural engineering at my disposal, and who has endeavoured to keep me on the straight and narrow path over many matters.

To my wife Elizabeth go my sincerest thanks for her tolerance of lonely evenings as a book widow. Without her forbearance there would simply have been no book.

All errors are much regretted and are entirely my own.

John Rapley

Introduction

With the 200th anniversary of the birth of Robert Stephenson on the horizon, a review of his part in the introduction of wrought iron as a major structural material seems timely. His adoption of wrought iron was not entirely from preference, for he regarded cast iron as a material of first choice, but it was forced on him from necessity. No other material had the capacity to provide the length of span required to carry the Chester & Holyhead Railway over the River Conwy and the Menai Strait. William Fairbairn, who partnered Stephenson in this ground-breaking enterprise, was himself neither a builder of bridges nor of railways, but his unrivalled knowledge of the properties and uses of iron complemented Stephenson's ability to manage major contracts. Together they proved invincible.

The decade from 1845 to 1855 was a period of momentous development in the use of iron for the construction of railway bridges, even though a financial crisis following the excesses of the Railway Mania of 1845-1847 delayed new work for several years. In 1845, wrought iron was to most engineers an unknown quantity and cast iron ruled supreme, though the great Joseph Locke favoured neither. Yet, a decade later, wrought iron dominated the field as it would continue to do for another forty years. Progress might have been swifter had the practising engineers not ignored or even despised the parallel work being done on structural theory by the mathematicians and academics. Unfortunately, in Britain during the following thirty years, the dominance of company engineers in an innately conservative profession tended to stifle innovation. Less inhibited were the consulting engineers working abroad, where they had freedom from the dead hand of the Railway Inspectorate of the Board of Trade, and in consequence were more willing to venture into new territory.

The acceptance by the Board of Trade in 1877 of the use of steel for bridges, albeit at a modest thirty per cent greater stress than for wrought iron, marked an important turning point, although again the reluctance to innovate by the more conservative engineers restricted its wider use. Furthermore, early experiments on the continent using Bessemer steel of doubtful quality had earned the material a bad name. Even in the United States, where engineers regarded themselves as being in the van of progress, the use of steel was slow to develop before 1880. In a leading article in *Engineering* of 17 December 1880, the editor commented with some prescience:

> *Rolled steel joists of the cheapest Belgian manufacture… will frequently break with considerably less than an inch deflection, whilst others of the same dimensions will fail to break under a foot deflection. Mere weight of rail or chair is no guarantee of security, especially in these days of steel, when a bad rail may fly into half-a-dozen pieces and lead to the death or mutilation of as many passengers.*

The Great Executive and the Great Empiricist

While the tubular beam was the greatest innovation in the earlier years of iron as a bridge building material, it proved to be short lived. In 1845, however the concept was new; the use of wrought iron as a major structural material was new; the mode of construction by assembling the tubes on land, floating them into position, and lifting them into place by hydraulic power was new; most importantly, the introduction of structural continuity to reduce the bending forces in the tube was practised for the first time with some degree of scientific understanding. The normally conventional Stephenson had deep misgivings along the way but if the Menai Strait was to be bridged he seemed to be left with little choice.

Before embarking on the history of the five known tubular bridges – those where the train was carried within the tube – a few words on the two engineers who dominated their design and building will not be out of place. There can be few to whom the name of Robert Stephenson is not familiar, but William Fairbairn, a far greater technologist, and without whose talents the Britannia Bridge as we knew it would never have been built, has been sadly underrated by the historians and biographers of the last 150 years.

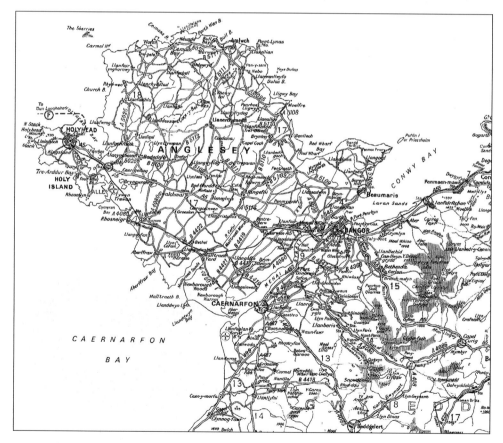

A general map of the area.

One

Stephenson and Fairbairn

Robert Stephenson, 1803-1859

A superabundance of biographies of Robert Stephenson has been published, both during his lifetime and in the century and a half since his death in 1859. Many have been mere pot-boilers, while others are of great merit. With the 200th anniversary of his birth falling in 2003, doubtless more will follow and the old familiar myths will be perpetuated. Most interested readers will be aware of at least the outlines of Robert Stephenson's rise from being the son of a Northumberland colliery enginewright, George Stephenson, to the highest eminence in the civil engineering profession, an outstanding executive of international fame, honoured with a tomb in Westminster Abbey.

As the boy developed, so too his father's fortunes improved, and Robert, after learning all that the village schoolmaster in Long Benton could teach him, moved to attend Dr Bruce's Percy Street Academy in Newcastle where he spent five years, riding to and fro daily on his donkey. Socially, this school was considered to be a cut above the Newcastle grammar school, and the delicate boy, for he took after his dead mother, with his pitman's speech and home-made clothes, must have suffered much among the sons

Robert Stephenson in later life.

of the professional men of the city. Despite this, he survived and the good general education which he received at Dr Bruce's was later to stand him in good stead. He does not seem to have profited greatly from his one session at Edinburgh University, except for first meeting there someone destined to be his lifelong friend and professional colleague – George Parker Bidder, son of a Devon stonemason, and possessing extraordinary powers of mental calculation and a penchant for legal matters.

After two years' apprenticeship to Nicholas Wood, the viewer or manager at Killingworth Colliery, Robert joined his father on the survey for the Stockton & Darlington Railway, afterwards leaving for a session at Edinburgh University until recalled by his father to assist with a survey for the proposed Liverpool & Manchester Railway. In studying natural philosophy, he found geology the science nearest to his heart. At the age of twenty, he was placed in charge of the newly opened locomotive works of Robert Stephenson & Co. in Newcastle. To broaden his horizons, if not to escape from a domineering parent, he then spent three years as a mining engineer in South America. On his return to the Forth Street Works, he became involved in the building of the locomotive which won the Rainhill Trials in 1829, *The Rocket*. In 1833, with the magic of the Stephenson name behind him, Robert was appointed engineer for the London & Birmingham Railway and, by 1844, even before the Railway Mania, he had become one a select band of major railway engineers.

William Fairbairn, 1789-1874

Fairbairn's life followed a rather different path, and was a true story of rags to riches in the best Victorian tradition. Born at Kelso in the Scottish Borders, where his father was a farmworker, the family moved to Conon Bridge in the Highlands where for two years he attended Mullochy School, receiving a general grounding aided by a generous application of the tawse – a leather strap. Three months were then spent with an uncle in Galashiels

A bust of William Fairbairn in his prime, around 1850.

Fairbairn's vertical lifting bridge on the North Docks branch of the Lancashire & Yorkshire Railway at Liverpool. Built about 1854, it crosses Regents Road and the fixed span on the left crossed the former route of the Liverpool Overhead Railway.

studying surveying and the Psalms in equal measure, but with this his formal education ended. Some time later his father was appointed farm manager by the proprietors of Percy Main Colliery near Newcastle, and the family moved south. Fairbairn was apprenticed to a millwright with whom he remained until the end of 1811. It was during this period that he first met George Stephenson, who was then in charge of a winding engine at Willington Quay.

After travelling as a journeyman to gain experience, Fairbairn settled in Manchester where, in 1818, he joined forces with James Lillie and by dint of hard work and innovation they prospered as millwrights, revolutionising many of the working practices. In 1824 they purchased a former iron foundry in Canal Street, Ancoats, and by 1830 were employing 300 men. In 1832 Fairbairn bought out Lillie's interest and started experiments with iron boats. In 1835 a shipyard was opened at Millwall on the Thames and in 1839 the Canal Street Works commenced the construction of locomotives. In 1837 Fairbairn and Eaton Hodgkinson, a Manchester scientist and mathematician, started experimental work on the properties of iron and the strength of riveted joints. Faced with a strike of boilermakers, Fairbairn devised a steam riveter, which was afterwards used at Menai. There followed a variety of work associated with the use of iron in machinery and structures, including the construction of a large cast iron woollen mill in Turkey, where much consultancy work followed. Thus, when Fairbairn first discussed the problems at Menai with Robert Stephenson in April 1844, he had a wealth of practical experience and theoretical knowledge behind him.

The Great Tubular Bridges

The story of the Britannia and Conwy tubular bridges has been told many times before, but it is well worth telling once again in order that Fairbairn's indispensable contribution may be afforded due prominence. Moreover, it offers the chance of a long overdue tribute to many other men who played their parts in building the greatest engineering wonders of the day.

Apart from a few authors alive at the time, none of whom were actually engaged in the project, the primary sources of information have always been two books. The more modest volume was published by Fairbairn in 1849, after his connection with the bridges had ceased, but in the following year Edwin Clark's imposing work (at three times the price) caught the public eye. Written with considerable help from his brother, Latimer, and under the watchful eye of Robert Stephenson, it combined an account of the bridges together with a textbook on structural engineering. The mathematical design and strength of materials' sections were contributed by William Pole FRS (1814-1900) at Stephenson's request, being somewhat beyond Clark's competence. Both these volumes, and much other invaluable reference material including Clark's working diary, have been carefully preserved in the archives of the Institution of Civil Engineers, where they can be inspected by appointment.

It is impossible to reconcile the two accounts completely but, from its somewhat pompous style and self-congratulatory tone, Clark's book lends credence to Fairbairn's acid comment, writing as a man who considered himself deeply wronged:

> It seems to have been got up for the praise of Stephenson and his school, claiming the merit of a great discovery, to which they have not a shadow of a title, beyond a very crude idea of a wrought iron suspended cylinder, which I afterwards proved to be useless.

Nonetheless, the list of subscribers contains many eminent names. Whatever their feelings, four members of the Fairbairn family ordered copies. John Weale, the publisher, took twenty-five, Stephenson himself ordered twenty and the contractors Charles Mare, and Easton and Amos who supplied the patented lifting chains, took ten each. In all, some 600 copies were ordered by subscription.

Fairbairn had a justifiable complaint that his contribution to the project was barely acknowledged and he himself had paid a generous tribute to Clark in his own book the year before. But there was a sting in its tail:

> I willingly bear my testimony to the great value of the services rendered by Mr Clarke [sic], to his talents, and to the great energy which he displayed in working out his several duties, but these had no reference whatever to the designing of the structure.

By way of contrast, Stephenson's views had been expressed in a speech at Conwy on 17 May 1848 after the opening of the first Conwy tube – the speech which precipitated Fairbairn's resignation as will be alluded to later. Clark, after two years in

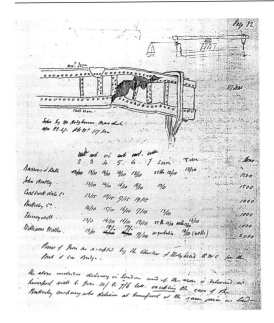

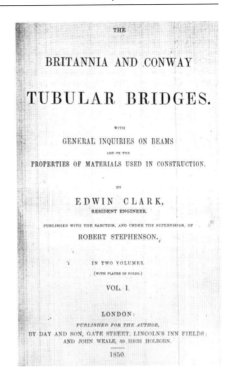

Above: Clark's diary.
Right: Clark's title page.

Stephenson's service, starting a year after the project commenced and after completion of the first series of experiments, was described in a newspaper report of the speech as:

> *A gentleman to whose talents, to whose zeal and ability, from the commencement of this undertaking, I am much indebted; and indeed the full development of the principles of tubular bridges is by no means in a small degree indebted to him – I allude to my assistant, Mr Edmund Clark [sic]. He has been my closet companion from the commencement of the preliminary investigation; no variation or inconsistency in the experiments eluded his keen perception; he was always on the lookout for contingencies that might effect the success – though not the principle, still the success – of the undertaking, and he and the gentlemen who I have just named, [i.e. Fairbairn and Hodgkinson] are the three to whom I feel deeply indebted for having brought the theory I first broached to such perfection.*

Clark, writing with the encouragement of Stephenson, attempted, unjustifiably but with a considerable degree of public success, to claim all the credit for his master and himself. Factual statements, where supported by clear evidence, can be accepted with some confidence, but the many unsupported assertions call for careful scrutiny and a considerable degree of scepticism. This applies equally to later accounts, which have in the main been based uncritically on Clark's work. Fairbairn's book is largely derived from correspondence between Stephenson, Eaton Hodgkinson and himself. Stephenson was furious at what he regarded as private letters being published, but they lent Fairbairn's account great authenticity, which Clark was less able to achieve.

The Training of Engineers in the 1840s

In the 1840s formal engineering training in the United Kingdom was gradually coming into vogue, though distrusted by the majority who had progressed the hard way as assistants or pupils of established engineers. Theoretical education was dismissed in favour of learning on the job. Many early engineers learnt their profession in the coal mining industry, a very rough and ready environment. Perhaps because so many came from the coalfields of the north east it was appropriate for the University of Durham to lead the way, followed by Kings College, London, in 1838 and Glasgow University shortly afterwards in 1840. Trinity College, Dublin, was next in 1841 and in the same year came the appointment of Charles Blacker Vignoles as Professor of Civil Engineering at University College, London. When questioned as to suitable subjects for the syllabus, Vignoles wrote:

> I would say that they should be strictly confined to pure Civil Engineering or the Art of Construction as distinguished from Decorative Architecture or more operative Mechanisms – of course avoiding all mathematics.

Coming from one of French extraction, well aware of the vastly superior technical education available in France, this is a rather extraordinary attitude, but reflects correctly the disdain with which theoretical training was treated in England at this period.

Timoshenko sums up the situation in the early nineteenth century:

> However, although English theoretical work on strength of materials was of such poor quality, British engineers had to solve many important engineering problems. The country was ahead of others in industrial development and the introduction of such materials as cast iron and wrought iron into structural and mechanical engineering presented many new problems and called for investigations of the mechanical properties of these new materials. A considerable amount of experimental work was completed and the results that were compiled found use not only in England but also in France.

The Application of Structural Continuity

One matter which will be dealt with later is the construction of the Britannia Bridge as a pair of continuous beams. The idea of using the shorter land spans as counterpoises to the main tubes obviously originated from an earlier proposal to use balanced cantilevers in order to obviate the need for scaffolding, but beyond that Clark is unfortunately silent as to who suggested and advised on the practical application of continuity. The adoption of this mode of construction proved crucial to the long term future of the bridge and it would appear that Clark himself may have first advocated it, although the credit may equally belong to his friend and colleague Charles Heard Wild. Fairbairn was far from fully convinced of its benefits, having designed his tubes as simple beams which he considered to be more than adequate. He did, of course, envisage physical continuity of the tubes from the beginning but, having carried out no experiments on structurally continuous beams, he would not commit himself. He remarked that mathematicians lived in a perfect world and faced with Pole's investigation of the two span Torksey Bridge, he made this sceptical comment:

> *I have given the above investigation of Mr Pole rather to stimulate experimental enquiry than to imply reliance on his conclusions. Mr Pole, it will be observed, attempts to prove that the strength of a continuous girder like that of the Torksey Bridge, extending over two spans, is to that of an independent girder as 3:2. Now the formula for this calculation may or may not be correct as the premises on which it is founded approach or recede from the truth; it is apparently, however, not derived from experiment, but from assumed data, which may be questioned in our attempts to reduce it to practice.*

Thus spoke the convinced empiricist – if not the last, perhaps the greatest of his kind in the field of bridge building. As each year passed, there came a greater understanding of how forces in a structure could be calculated or at least estimated and how iron and other materials would behave under stress. Credit is generally accorded to James Barton, a former pupil of Sir John Macneill, for the first scientifically designed open web triangulated girder in the Boyne Viaduct at Drogheda, Ireland. It was not until 1856, however, when Jourawski's pioneering work on Howe trusses in Russia was published in France, that a full understanding of the forces in the webs of girders became more widely known, and in due course this knowledge found its way to England.

A Meeting of Great Minds

Brief mention has been made of William Fairbairn's early life prior to the time he became involved with Stephenson in the tubular bridges. He was not an ironmaster in the general sense of being a primary producer. Rather he was a master of iron, with an accumulated knowledge of the production and working of the material which few, if any, of the traditional ironmasters could match. The foundry at his Canal Street works could handle castings up to 35 tons in weight, but wrought iron sections and plates were bought in as required. This practical expertise was backed up by extensive experimental work to establish strength and properties of cast and wrought iron columns and riveted joints. In this Fairbairn worked closely with Eaton Hodgkinson, another Manchester man, whose mathematical ability proved invaluable in establishing empirical formulae.

It was just such a man that Stephenson needed for advice on the practicability of constructing the huge iron tubes proposed for Menai, and they must have been little acquainted or he would surely have approached Fairbairn sooner. With no precedents for guidance, and with the limited theory understood or even valued by practising engineers, this was by any standards a major undertaking. Structural theory was in any case still at an early stage of development and a wide gulf separated the practical engineers from those academics like Henry Moseley who, if consulted, were in a position to offer advice and guidance. To a large extent they existed on different planes, unlike the position in France and Germany, and too many early British engineers were contemptuous of their more intellectual colleagues.

Chance played a part in the initial meeting between Robert Stephenson and Fairbairn. For many years, since their days on the Tyne, Fairbairn and George Stephenson had been firm friends. In 1804 Fairbairn entered into a seven-year apprenticeship as a mechanical engineer at Percy Main Colliery where his father, Andrew, managed the farming interests of the proprietors. It was here that he first made the acquaintance of George Stephenson, eight years his senior, who was in charge of a steam engine at the nearby Willington Ballast Quay. Despite the age difference, the two men became firm friends, sharing a passion for things mechanical and an enthusiasm for self-education. Their love of the sport of wrestling was echoed in a letter from George in 1847 when he was sixty-six and near the end of his life. It is worth quoting:

Now for the challenge to wrestle. Had you not known that I had given up that species of sport, your durst not have made the expressions in your letter that you have done. Although you are a much taller and stronger man than myself, I am quite sure that I could have smiled in your face when you were laying on your back! I know your wife would not like to see me do this, therefore let me have no more boasting, or you might get the worst of it.

Although George had retired to Tapton House, Chesterfield, in 1840 to pursue his industrial and agricultural interests, he made periodical forays to London and the Stephensons' offices at 24 Great George Street, Westminster. There, Robert kept his father informed of his activities in which the old man was greatly interested and sometimes still able to offer useful advice. It was probably on just such a visit in the spring of 1844 that Fairbairn called to talk over old times and found himself cornered by Robert. By this time Robert was convinced that his suspended tube offered the only solution at Menai, but he was desperately anxious for knowledgeable advice. Fairbairn could see the possibilities of the tubular construction, but protested that he could not offer a considered opinion without experimental work. Agreement was speedily reached for Fairbairn to carry out a series of tests on various tube shapes at his Millwall yard, subject to the approval of the Board of the Chester & Holyhead Railway. In due course this approval was forthcoming, and the then considerable sum of £3,000 was voted to cover expenses.

The Men and the Bridges

The civil engineering department of the Chester & Holyhead Railway was formed along the lines which Stephenson had so successfully pioneered on the London & Birmingham Railway. At the top of the pyramid was Robert Stephenson himself, based at his offices in Westminster, where the day-to-day running was entrusted to John Sanderson, his brother-in-law and confidant. The railway company had its offices in the

City of London in Moorgate, where the company secretary, George King, played a leading part in the administrative business. The chairman was George Carr Glyn, often regarded as the railway banker because of his extensive interests. The directors were all busy men, with more of an eye on the anticipated profits than anxious to get their expensive boots dirty, so little time was spent by them in visiting the works in progress. Since the board and the engineer-in-chief were so far from North Wales, they appointed one of their number, Capt. Constantine Richard Moorsom RN, as resident director based at Bangor. For Stephenson the days of 'living on the line', as he had done on his first major railway, were long gone and his heavy workload allowed only limited site visits, though he claimed to have walked the line fifteen times during construction. The journalist F.R. Conder summed up the situation:

> *The politics of the line, so to speak, occupied the Engineer-in-Chief far more anxiously than did the actual engineering questions. The filling-up of the share list, the management of the directory, and perhaps the check-mating of the secretary, made imperative demands on the time of the Engineer of a projected line.*

Conder overlooked one of the most onerous duties, that of preparing the Bill for piloting through the parliamentary scrutiny. This could be a demanding duty occupying hours, days, weeks and occasionally months, depending on the degree of the often virulent opposition. Whereas George Stephenson had faced humiliation at the hands of a clever lawyer in 1825, Robert and his partner Bidder were capable of dealing blow for blow but the loss of a Bill meant not only delay but much time and capital uselessly expended before even a yard of track could be laid.

In the 1845 Session Stephenson was fortunate and, meeting little opposition, the C&H No.2 Bill was approved in a few days. In all, 120 Bills were successful in 1845 and 272 the following year when the Railway Mania was at its height. As far as possible, Bills liable to fall by the wayside were weeded out in advance to relieve the pressure. An extreme case in the 1845 Session was the London & York Bill, which fell after seventy days in committee. Its consulting engineer, Sir William Cubitt, must have had a strong constitution.

This would have been bad enough in the ordinary course of events, but conditions in 1845 can only be described as atrocious by any civilised standard. The Palace of Westminster was under reconstruction and, in consequence, the so called Committee Rooms were no better than temporary wooden sheds. It was a long hot summer and the stifling heat inside was helped little by throwing buckets of water on the roof. The Great Stink of 1858 was still to come, but thirteen years earlier the Thames was already an open sewer and had been for many years. The sewage was carried out to sea with one tide only to return as the tide rose, the current depositing its unsavoury contents on the wide mud banks. It was this foul soup which young Isambard Brunel had to swim through when the river burst into the Thames Tunnel, and the wonder is that he survived. In 1845 Mr Mitchell, an experienced committee clerk, remarked that the smell would never be effaced from his memory.

The Hierarchy of Engineers

Initially two resident engineers were appointed, both well known to Stephenson and much respected. Alexander Ross had charge of the line from Chester to Conwy, and Frank Forster from Conwy to Holyhead. Purists may argue that to speak of Frank shows an unseemly familiarity, but Frank he appears to have been to all his colleagues, as a subscriber to Clark's book, and even to his official obituarist. So Frank he shall remain! Perhaps the Victorians were not quite so stuffy in their daily lives as we have been led to believe. To the contrary, F.R. Conder writes wistfully, from his personal experience, of the fun enjoyed by the junior engineers – below the assistants were the sub-assistants who for long periods could be out in the field and subject to little supervision by their superiors.

After Fairbairn's resignation in 1848, Edwin Clark, who until then had been his assistant, was appointed resident engineer for the construction of the tubes and their erection, and he had the able assistance of his brother, Latimer; perhaps time would show who was the better engineer of the two. His Superintendent of Ironwork was John McLaren, assisted by Charles Rolfe, whose presence of mind was destined to save the day during the floating out of the first Britannia tube. Responsibility for stations and the smaller bridges was delegated to Charles Heard Wild, an up-and-coming young engineer who had started his career as a draughtsman on the Manchester & Birmingham Railway, under the respected George W. Buck. His assistant was one George Grove, who was later to turn to music and to distinguish himself as the author of *Grove's Dictionary of Music and Musicians*, of which a new edition has recently been published. Finally, Hedworth Lee, originally assistant to Ross, was placed in charge of the permanent way, and in 1851 had the honour of conducting the Duke of Wellington over both tubular bridges. Later, in 1857, Lee was appointed District Engineer by the LNWR.

So far not mentioned, but playing a most indispensable part, was the architect Francis Thompson. His position was that of a consultant and not an employee as the others were, but close supervision of the masonry contractors and the builders of the magnificent joint station at Chester fell to his lot. C.H. Wild is credited by *Parry's Guide* with the design of the large iron train shed at Chester.

Several of these men had started their careers under Stephenson and were intensely loyal to 'The Chief', with many on terms of personal friendship and not mere underlings. Their parts will become clearer as the story unfolds. The hallmark of Stephenson's system was his practice to delegate responsibility down to the lowest practicable level and, in contrasting his methods with the centralised and autocratic organisation operated by Brunel, Conder wrote:

> The staff of Mr Stephenson … to some extent resembled an army corps in division and subordination of duty. Each officer was the servant of the Company. Each had his own limit of function and responsibility; and although Mr Stephenson well knew how to show, from time to time, that not the smallest detail would escape his attention, if it involved what was wrong, the order of his office was not such as to overburden the Engineer-in-Chief with details that fell properly within the competence of the residents, or even of the Subs.

Although he will appear later in the account of the Dee Bridge failure, Maj.-Gen. Sir Charles William Pasley FRS (1780-1861) deserves more than a passing mention. By 1840, the increasing number of railway accidents resulted in a public outcry for some sort of Government control. Too many of the early companies gave priority to the interests of shareholders, and subsequent railway history records fiercely fought rearguard actions against such measures as improved signalling and continuous brakes. The first Inspector was appointed in 1840 and Maj.-Gen. Pasley took up his post in 1842, after a distinguished military career in Spain and the Low Countries. On the retreat from Corunna he gave his horse to a wounded soldier and carried on, on foot with only one boot. He started the School of Military Engineering at Chatham in 1812 and was its Director until 1841, becoming a Fellow of the Royal Society in 1816. He was prominent in underwater demolition work and the use of explosives. All but one of the Inspectors up to 1892 were drawn from the officers of the Royal Engineers on account of their broad knowledge of engineering matters but above all for their integrity and impartiality. Today railway safety is in the experienced hands of career civil servants.

Two

In the Beginning: the Rocky Road to Dublin

From the earliest times, communications between England and Ireland had been difficult. Ireland lacked the resources to improve them and England lacked the will. Finally the Act of Union, passed by both the British and the Irish Parliaments in May 1800, led to the centralisation of all political power in Westminster as from 1 January 1801, and brought to the fore the urgent necessity for greatly improved transport. That it took another fifty years to fully achieve this was largely due to the primitive state of transport technology at the beginning of the nineteenth century, compounded by procrastination by those in London who held the purse strings. While this state of affairs was allowed to continue the perils and discomforts of crossing the Irish Sea in small boats, having braved the Menai ferry, were the greatest obstacles to political and economic integration.

Liverpool and Dublin were then the principal ports, although Dublin existed as a port more in name than in fact. Unfortunate travellers were decanted, weather permitting, at the Pigeon House Quay on a sand bar at the mouth of the Liffey in Dublin Bay. The 122 miles of notoriously stormy crossing in quite small sailing boats were not to be undertaken lightly by the fainthearted. The study of a map showed that the distance

Thomas Telford is generally acknowledged as the father of modern civil engineering; he has also been described as the greatest bridge-builder and road-maker that the world has ever known.

Telford's Menai Bridge.

could be halved if a harbour was constructed on the Welsh coast on the shores of Anglesey. At that time, however, there was wild and largely undeveloped country west of Shrewsbury and through Snowdonia, and the coast road was roundabout with an additional short but sometimes perilous ferry at Conwy. From Shrewsbury to London the route was by way of Watling Street which had been greatly improved after the passing of the Turnpike Act of 1751.

The ferries at Menai and Conwy presented hazardous crossings in rough weather, while animals had to be swum across at all times of the year; accidents and drowning were not uncommon. On Christmas Day, 1806, the *Annual Register* reported: 'Owing to a heavy swell in the River Conway [*sic*], the boat conveying the Irish Mail and eight passengers and seven other persons was upset, only two persons being saved.'

Any improvements were strenuously opposed by the Liverpool shipping interests, fearful of losing a virtual monopoly of the lucrative trade across the Irish Sea. But in 1802, having endured a winter struggling between their constituencies and Westminster, a group of Irish Members of Parliament complained so vociferously as to succeed in bringing a promise of action from Viscount Sidmouth, the Tory Prime Minister of the day. John Rennie and Capt. Joseph Huddart were instructed to investigate and report on an improved sea route. They favoured a new harbour at Holyhead on the north west corner of Anglesey, together with a new road from Shrewsbury to Bangor, with a ferry across the Menai Strait to Anglesey, and also recommended the construction of harbours at Howth and Kingstown (Dun Laoghaire) in the vicinity of Dublin. There, for seven years, the matter rested until the election of a new Government in 1809 when, at last, Parliament voted sufficient finds for the work to start. No action was taken at that time to improve the appalling state of the road west from Shrewsbury, nor to address the inconvenient necessity for a ferry across the narrow but often turbulent Menai Strait.

In 1808, the Postmaster General had taken a hand in the matter, but his attempt to improve the mail service was defeated by the primitive state of the road, where in one week three post horses suffered broken legs. As a Mr William Akers complained to a Committee of the House of Commons:

> *Stagecoaches have been frequently overturned and broken from the badness of the road, and mails have been overturned; but I wonder that more and worse accidents have not occurred from the badness of the road.*

Losing all patience after another six years of inaction, the redoubtable Sir Henry Parnell MP, for Queens County, complained bitterly of the wretched state of the road after his own coach had been overturned and its passengers plunged into a pool of water. His intervention led to the setting up of the Holyhead Road Commission, which instructed the famous road builder, Thomas Telford, to survey the whole route from London to Holyhead. Telford's new road, which remains in use today, was a remarkable feat, passing through the heart of Snowdonia by way of Betws-y-coed to Bangor.

At Holyhead the first harbour works were commenced in 1810 under the direction of John Rennie Senior but were not completed until 1824, and these were followed twenty years later by the much larger harbour of refuge carried out by James Meadows Rendel (1799-1856) where the railway pier is situated. The opening of Telford's magnificent

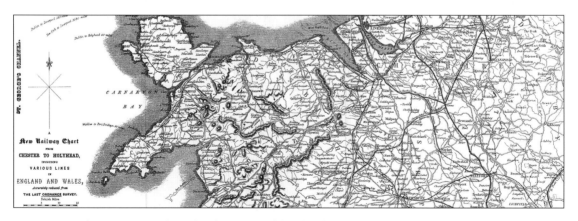

A map from *Parry's Guide to the Chester & Holyhead Railway*.

Telford's suspension bridge at Menai with its pioneering span of 579ft. It was strengthened in the Second World War.

suspension bridges at Menai and Conwy early in 1826 finally allowed mail coaches to run through to Holyhead without the inconvenience, and danger, of ferries. Steamers had been introduced in 1819 at the same time as the new harbour at Howth was opened, and the reliability of the service became much improved in consequence. No longer were boats delayed, sometimes for days, by contrary winds and tides. For a time at least the opposition to the Holyhead route remained undiminished. However, until 1838 it was frustrated by the absence of a direct railway route between Liverpool and London. For a while after the coming of the railway, the mail contract returned to Liverpool and it was only after completion of the Chester & Holyhead Railway with the opening of the Britannia Bridge in March 1850 that Holyhead came into its own again, despite continuing competition from Liverpool.

The Coming of the Railways

The benefits of a short sea crossing were not overlooked, and in 1836 the Irish Railway Commission was set up, with Charles Blacker Vignoles as its engineer. The attractions of Holyhead were clear enough, but the problem of crossing the Menai Strait demanded a practical solution. In 1838, Francis Giles proposed a route skirting the North Wales coast, with a single line of railway on the deck of Telford's Bridge. Coaches and wagons would be hauled across one at a time by horses, although the use of a steam engine and ropes was not ruled out. Asked to report on this scheme at the end of 1838, George Stephenson generally supported Giles' proposals, although he favoured several deviations to reduce the costs of tunnelling. He appears, and for very good reason, to have had misgivings about using Telford's bridge, but without offering any firm proposals for an alternative. Initially his son, Robert, also considered the use of the suspension bridge but only as a last resort, as well it might have proved.

Telford's bridge had been found decidedly lively under the influence of winds funnelled by the narrow gorge and on many occasions horses, as well as passengers, refused to cross. Deck movement during construction was a frequent problem, and only a week after opening a storm did considerable damage. Equally serious damage was done a fortnight later, and Telford was almost at his wits' end. Even after strengthening, the movement of the deck continued to cause concern and, during a hurricane in 1839, 175ft of the deck was destroyed and other major damage occurred; though by great good fortune the chains held. It was common knowledge that on more than one occasion the mail coach had been overturned by the movement of the bridge. One guard reported:

> *Twenty minutes lost at the Bridge it blowing hard and the Bridge in great motion, which caused the horses to fall all down together and be entangled in each other's harness. Had to set them at liberty one at a time by cutting the harness.*

Vignoles was not a man to be deterred easily and was considerably more open-minded about new developments than most of his contemporaries, but even he regarded a railway bridge at Menai as being out of the question. A site for a new harbour on the coast south of Caernarfon was found in a small cove, sheltered from the prevailing winds, at Porthdynllaen, close to the village of Nefyn and a few miles west of Pwllheli. Several alternative routes for a railway were put forward, but Vignoles preferred a line west from Shrewsbury to Llangollen and Bala, and through Dolgellau to the coast at Barmouth. From there, it followed the coast to Porthmadog and Pwllheli, a circuitous route with heavy gradients through the mountains.

A treasury committee was appointed in November 1839 to examine and report on the competing lines, and early in 1840 they came out strongly in favour of George Stephenson's line from Chester to Holyhead. Apart from preferring this route for its own virtues, they were strongly influenced by the availability of the existing harbour at Holyhead. Alternative schemes for a new harbour at Ormes Bay (Llandudno) and an extension of the north coast line from Bangor to Porthdynllaen were also ruled out by two Admiralty Inspectors in January 1840. The ground was now clear for the promotion of the Chester & Holyhead Railway, but a means of crossing the Menai Strait still had to be found and no practicable schemes were forthcoming. This was a matter in which the Admiralty showed a great deal of concern and, acting in defence of navigational interests, they would have the final word on any bridge proposed.

By 1840 Chester had a direct line to London by way of Crewe and Birmingham but the times were not propitious for further development due to one of the many trade recessions that plagued Victorian commerce. A boom and bust economy was already well established, quite apart from such lunacies as the Railway Mania of 1845-1846. This did not inhibit the proliferation of committees and the submission of report after report. June 1842 also saw the appointment of a Select Committee of the House of Commons to examine the state of Post Office communication with Ireland. Having gone over much the same ground as before, their decision favoured the North Wales coast route from Chester to Holyhead.

In May 1843 the Admiralty appointed two naval officers as inspectors, and they too favoured Holyhead. The following October, James Walker, the eminent civil engineer, who had been asked by the Admiralty for his observations, was somewhat noncommittal in his report and saw advantages in the Vignoles scheme. By the end of the year the North Wales & Dublin Railway & Harbour Co. was established to revive the Ormes Bay scheme, or an alternative port at Conwy, but like its predecessors it was to quietly fade away.

As far back as March 1839, a prospectus had been issued for the Great Holyhead Railway. The financial crisis of 1840 was such that in the parliamentary session that year no Acts for new railways were passed. Somewhere down the line, the GHR metamorphosed into the Chester & Holyhead Railway. 1841 saw the height of the depression, and it was not until November 1843 that the promoters of the CHR were in a position to seek an Act of Incorporation. In due course the CHR Bill was first read in the Commons in March 1844 and received the Royal Assent in July of that year, with Robert Stephenson designated as Chief Engineer. A short section of line, including the Conwy and Menai crossings, was omitted to allow detailed plans for the bridges to be submitted in the following session.

In the session of 1845, the CHR No.2 Bill was due to come up for parliamentary scrutiny and Stephenson was left with little time to prepare firm proposals for the bridges. Should he fail to put forward workable schemes the Bill would fail and progress would be delayed for yet another year. By the beginning of April 1845, he had only a half-formed idea of a tube suspended from chains, and it was fortunate that his chance meeting with William Fairbairn saved the day. Nothing like it had ever been proposed before, but Fairbairn's expertise lay in his knowledge of the working of wrought iron, particularly in its application to ship building. In 1845 wrought iron was an almost unknown quantity in the building of bridges.

British Iron Bridges Before 1845

Abraham Darby's graceful cast-iron arch over the Severn at Coalbrookdale, with a span of 100ft, was completed in 1779, the first major bridge to be built entirely of iron. It was followed some years later by Telford's Buildwas Bridge of 1796, a few miles upstream,

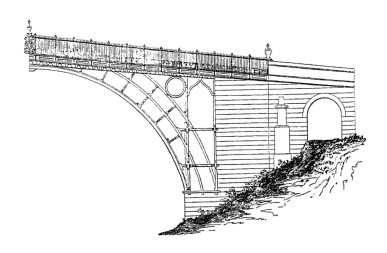

The Iron Bridge, Coalbrookdale, over the River Severn, was built to the order of Abraham Darby III in 1779. It had a semicircular arch spanning 100ft.

which had a span of 130ft. In design, its build was the forerunner of the cast-iron arch rather than Darby's pioneering concept, which was based on the mode of construction of timber bridges and was in fact designed by an architect. By 1845 the cast-iron arch had become well established and it was only to be expected that Stephenson would turn first to such well-tried and reliable form of construction. Unfortunately he had reckoned without Capt. Alexander Vidal and the Admiralty – a factor that will be explained later.

The simple cast-iron beam, immensely popular for small spans, had reached its practical limit of around 50ft. The Midland & Great Western Railway of Ireland had built a bridge of this size in 1845, with girders of 52ft, each cast in one piece. Trussed cast-iron girders, which were within a short time to be condemned as structurally objectionable, had not yet been built for a span as great as 100ft. Clearly any form of cast-iron beam was impracticable at Menai.

To George Stephenson, and to his contractors, John & Isaac Burrell of Newcastle, must go the credit for the first all-iron trussed railway bridge. Earlier iron bridges on tramways had been merely simple iron beams, but Stephenson's little bridge over the River Gaunless on the Stockton & Darlington Railway, opened in 1825, was far more sophisticated than its resemblance to a giant bedstead may suggest. It had three spans of 12ft 6in each, and a fourth was added a year later to reduce flooding. Structurally it had much in common with Brunel's Saltash Bridge, opened thirty-four years later and having spans thirty-six times as great, except that the Gaunless Bridge had a solid iron bottom chord instead of Brunel's chain.

The light construction of the Gaunless Bridge supports the assertion that it was never used by locomotives, though it carried horse-drawn traffic until the time of its rebuilding in 1901. After 1858, railway passenger traffic was diverted by another route. Is it too fanciful to suggest that, when Brunel made a sightseeing tour of the north east, at the end of 1831, a sight of the Gaunless Bridge could have sown a seed in his mind? Thanks to the foresight of the NER, who ensured its preservation, the Gaunless Bridge can still be studied in the National Railway Museum.

Small though it might be, the Gaunless Bridge was of a remarkably sophisticated design, showing an understanding of the parts in tension and the parts under compression. The appropriate material, wrought and cast iron respectively, was selected accordingly. It would seem likely that the Burrells with their practical knowledge must have made a contribution.

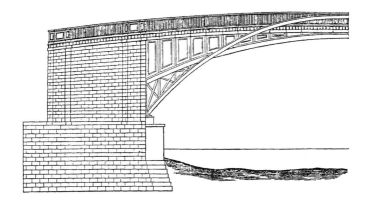

Thomas Telford's more sophisticated arch over the River Severn at Buildwas was built in 1796 with a span of 130ft but it was less than half the weight of the Iron Bridge.

The first iron railway bridge – George Stephenson's bridge over the River Gaunless at West Auckland, Co. Durham, built in 1825 by the contractors John & Isaac Burrell of Newcastle. It was dismantled 1901 and is now at York.

The Cast-Iron Tied Arch

On the London & Birmingham Railway, opened in 1838, Robert Stephenson introduced, probably for the first time, tied arches, designed by Charles Fox, for two major bridges – one over the Regent's Canal, and the other at Weedon which lasted in service until 1932. The principle of these was identical to the arches used on the High Level Bridge at Newcastle upon Tyne, where the deck ties together the ends of the arch and relieves any horizontal thrust. Three similar bridges were constructed by Thomas Gooch on the Manchester and Leeds line, of which that at Gauxholme with a span of 101ft remains in service, although the weight of traffic is now taken by steel girders inserted between the original cast-iron arches in 1905. The arches are built up from a series of heavy castings, but in the absence of diagonal bracing there is a tendency for the arch to distort under rolling loads, much as will be described later for timber arches but to a far lesser extent. To reduce this effect top weight was added above the arch, resulting in a very heavy structure.

Cast and Wrought Iron

A brief note on the differences in the manufacture and properties of cast iron and wrought iron may not be out of place. In both cases, the raw iron was smelted in a blast furnace, and the molten iron run into moulds in the floor resembling a sow with piglets – hence the name pig iron. With or without refining, pig iron could be melted and poured into moulds, which allowed the formation of intricate shapes in one operation. Unfortunately, such castings tend to be brittle and unreliable in tension but possess great resistance to

29

Cast-iron arches at Menai.

compression. Fairbairn was right to describe cast iron as a treacherous material when used in tension or subjected to shock loads, particularly at low temperatures.

Wrought iron was produced by refining pig iron in a puddling furnace, from which it was extracted in blooms of several hundredweight and hammered by a water-powered tilt hammer, or later Nasmyth's steam hammer, into a rough shape which could be further formed in a rolling mill to give various shapes such as round and flat bars, and angle and tee irons. This quality was known as merchant bar. By a further process of cutting round merchant bar into short lengths laid together, reheating and hammering them into a solid mass before re-rolling, a better quality iron was obtained, more suitable for plates. This was known as 'best' iron. Repeating the process once or twice again produced 'best best' and 'best best best' iron. The last was mainly used for boilerplates, but at Britannia it was specified for the bottoms of the tubes where they came under the greatest tensile stress.

In 1845, wrought iron was still in its infancy as a bridge-building material. It was expensive, very roughly twice the price of cast iron, and complex shapes could only be formed by fabrication which in those days meant riveting, forging or hammer welding. But it had great tensile strength and resistance to shock loads. The ship builders had long recognised its virtues, but the bridge engineers were slow to appreciate its potential. Joseph Locke was very critical of the use of iron of any kind for bridges, although in later life and under the influence of his partner, John Errington, his views mellowed. Nonetheless, his lines from Lancaster to Aberdeen were built without iron bridges. The effect was not entirely happy as a description of their Stirling Bridge shows.

The bridge over the Forth at Stirling had timber arches on stone piers, and these helped to provide some of the stiffness lacking in the arches. The effect of a train passing over it, after it had been in use for several years, was graphically described by Capt. Wynne RE, who was observing from the comparative safety of a new iron bridge nearby. His words were recorded in G. Drysdale Dempsey's book, *The Practical Railway Engineer*, published in 1855:

> *When the girder comes under the influence of a rolling weight, the haunch of the arch which is first affected becomes depressed, and the crown and the opposite haunch rise; as the weight rolls on, these parts become gradually depressed and the first part is elevated; the rolling body in fact produces a wave, which it drives before it until the wave has reached its maximum elevation, when it begins to recede passing back under the rolling weight…*

Locke built similar short-lived timber arches on the Woodhead line at Dinting Vale and Etherow. These became so decrepit that passengers refused to cross. Train crews must have been made of sterner stuff and were in those days, presumably, deemed expendable. As a general rule, brick or masonry arches were the engineers' first choice, all things being equal, but cast-iron arches were a cheaper substitute and hundreds if not thousands continue to give good service at, for example, the High Level Bridge at Newcastle upon Tyne, or elsewhere on the East Coast main line at Peterborough. However even cast-iron arches have their limitations, and a bridge built in 1839 by C.B. Vignoles reached the stage sixty years later where the piers were visibly rocking as the arches flexed under a train of more than twice the weight the designer had envisaged. Vignoles was reported to have complained that every time he designed a bridge, the engineers would come up with heavier locomotives.

The fundamental problem with arches was the headroom they required, and the greater the span the greater the problem. Engineers were forced to seek alternatives and to maintain a flat soffit. Tied arches offered one solution but they were clumsy and expensive, and they attempted, successfully at first, to extend the span of cast-iron girders by casting the girders in two or three sections, bolted together, and with wrought-iron tendons to resist the tension forces in the bottom flange. The idea had been developed in factory and mill buildings, although not without accident, and in 1832, Vignoles, ever in the van of progress, constructed two trussed bridges of 45ft span, cast in two sections, across the Leeds & Liverpool Canal.

For a couple of years the idea lay dormant until it was revived by George Parker Bidder for use on the Northern & Eastern Railway which eventually reached Cambridge. On the first stretch out of London, it was necessary to cross the Lea Navigation in the vicinity

The Royal Canal Bridge at Dublin.

England's first lattice girder viaduct at Bolton on the former Liverpool & Bury Railway. It was designed by James Thomson and opened in 1848. When rebuilt around 1881 the original main girders were retained as parapet girders and it is these 1848 girders which are visible.

of Tottenham. A two-part trussed girder bridge was erected and gave every satisfaction, at least for a while. The crunch came when one girder failed. Until the break was noticed, trains continued to cross without incident, the wrought-iron tendons supporting the cracked girder. In due course, the faulty casting was replaced, and little interest was shown in the cause of its failure. It was just one of those things that castings did from time to time.

Next Bidder built a three-section bridge over the Minories in the City of London for the London & Blackwall Railway, with a span of 63ft and what looked like a house on top in order that nervous horses in the street below should not be disturbed by the sudden appearance of moving trains overhead. The railway was cable operated in its early years so the bridge was lightly loaded and gave no problems. During the next few years some forty bridges of this type were planned or built, and the spans gradually increased. It was the failure of the Dee Bridge in May 1847 with five deaths that led to a Royal Commission and the end of the trussed girder. Thirteen others had been planned by John Hawkshaw for the Manchester South Junction & Altrincham Railway. Three were already built, but were replaced by cast-iron arches, as were ten awaiting construction. Today only one trussed girder remains in service, and that is for an aqueduct carrying the Cromford Canal over the Derby to Matlock line. The Dee Bridge affair is another story to be told later.

The most significant development took place in Ireland soon after 1840. Sir John Macneill (c.1793-1880), assisted by James Thomson, had built an experimental road bridge of 84ft span at Rahenny to cross the Dublin & Drogheda Railway then under construction. This was based on Ithiel Town's American patents of 1820 and 1835, which were intended originally for timber construction. The sides of Town's bridge were trussed by the use of a lattice or trellis of small timbers crossing approximately at right angles. Macneill adopted this idea but used flat bridges of 144ft span to cross the Royal Canal near Dublin and a city street. Unfortunately this pioneering design was not without its problems but is generally regarded as being the first true wrought-iron lattice bridge.

Elsewhere in Europe, timber remained the predominant material, although Russia and Sweden had well-developed wrought iron industries producing material of excellent quality. However, like America, they too had almost boundless supplies of cheap timber, and iron bridges were consequently slow to develop. In Russia much early development work was done on Howe trusses and it was there that the forces in open webs were first evaluated. But nowhere was there anything remotely approaching in scale the conditions Stephenson had to overcome at Menai. The only existing bridges of comparable span were all of the suspension type and their unsuitability for railway work was manifest to all as Capt. Samuel Brown's bridge at Stockton-on-Tees would prove.

An Innovative Solution

Stephenson considered but rejected several schemes for which there was no precedent. His first plan was for a pair of cast-iron arches, each of 350ft span, with the centre pier on the Britannia Rock. Strong objections were raised by the Admiralty, who demanded a clearance of 105ft similar to that afforded by Telford's suspension bridge nearby. Moreover, the Admiralty had received reports from Sir John Rennie, J.M. Rendel and Capt. Vidal RN insisting that this clearance had to be maintained over both navigable channels, giving a clear width of not less than 450ft. Nor would they allow any obstruction of the navigation by scaffolding during construction. An earlier scheme, suggested by Telford, to erect a single arch by building half arches out from the shore, tied back by

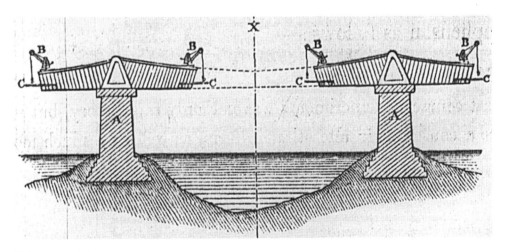

Balanced cantilevers.

Sunderland Bridge.

cables until they met at the centre, was impracticable with a pair of arches. An attempt to build a bridge at Sunderland on this principle by Burdon and Wilson had not succeeded without some scaffolding in the river-bed.

A modification of this scheme was considered, where the land arches were replaced with iron, so as to allow the bridge to be constructed as three balanced cantilevers, with expansion joints where the cantilevers met at mid-channel, but this too was ruled out because the headroom could not be maintained. In Stephenson's mind there arose the conjecture of how a suspension bridge could be modified to maintain the required rigidity in the deck essential for railway use. Working along these lines his thoughts turned to the concept of an iron tube, hung from chains and sufficiently large internally to allow the passage of a train.

As so often happens, others were later to lay claim to having originated the idea. Among them was Stephenson's colleague, James M. Rendal, who had supported the idea before the Parliamentary Committee, and a particularly importunate individual from Liverpool, who would continue to press his claim for years to come. There is no way of telling if his idea created a spark in Stephenson's mind which he adopted quite unconsciously as his own. A Frenchman, Dr Jules Guyot, protested at a meeting of the British Association in Edinburgh that the tubular bridge was his brainchild and that it was being stolen by perfidious English engineers. To his credit, William Fairbairn, even after his dispute with Stephenson, acknowledged the latter's claim to priority.

John De La Haye, a citizen of Liverpool, had approached Stephenson early in 1845 with a proposal for a submerged tube tunnel. This took the form of a watertight iron tube, which could be floated out and sunk into the bed of a river or another waterway to be crossed. After divers had joined the sections it would be pumped out and the tunnel completed. While the concept of the passage of a train through a tube was common, De La Haye's project bore little resemblance to Stephenson's tube suspended on chains. Fate decreed that the tubular bridge would be obsolescent within ten years of its conception, while the submerged tunnel proposal has stood the test of time. Its first recorded use was planned for T.W. Rammell's Waterloo & Whitehall Railway of 1865.

The first 200ft section of the tube was floated up river from Samuda's shipyard at Poplar and sunk onto concrete supports in the bed of the Thames. An unusually serious financial crisis arose in 1866, following the failure of Overend & Gurney's bank, and the tube was ignominiously refloated and towed away for scrap. Yet this was far from being a hare-brained scheme and, given more propitious circumstances, may well have succeeded. When yet a third road crossing was needed at Conwy, it is interesting to note that a submerged tube tunnel was chosen. John De La Haye was vindicated.

False claims and impractical ideas were the bane of the well-known names in engineering and Robert Stephenson suffered more than most. He found it particularly galling when his eminent colleague Rendel headed the queue purporting to have conceived the tubular bridge. Exasperated by this he wrote to Fairbairn on 26 October 1846:

> *I fear I am in a fair way of losing even a little credit for the introduction of tubular bridges … I am really desirous of avoiding a controversy on this matter, but I perceive it will be inevitable if such malicious and selfish rumours are set afloat, Mr Rendel had nothing to do whatever with the original idea: It was entirely my own.*

Stephenson's anger was understandable, and Fairbairn wrote back sympathetically the following day from Manchester:

> *I am much obliged by your letter of yesterday, and particularly that part of it which related to the original idea of the bridge, I was sure it was yours in every respect; but there is nothing new, or likely to turn out valuable but there immediately start up a hundred claimants. We are all subject to this species of mental encroachment; but in your case every-thing is now clear and no person can possibly establish a prior claim.*

This was all very well, but Fairbairn diplomatically ignored another crucial claim made by Stephenson in the same letter, which was to sow the first seed in an increasingly bitter dispute, which inevitably led to a rift between the two men. This was Stephenson's claim to have planned a bridge having a deck of cellular construction and intended to carry the Cambridge turnpike road over the Lea Navigation at Ware, thus predating Fairbairn's cellular concept by some months. Just how much substance this claim had is difficult to determine, since the bridge was never built in that form. Local folk memory attributes the long vanished bridge at that point to George Stephenson, though at the date of building he was in a well-earned retirement at Tapton House, Chesterfield.

Mention has already been made of William Fairbairn and his serendipitous encounter with Robert Stephenson at his office in Great George Street. Within a month of his first meeting with Fairbairn, Stephenson was called upon to give evidence to the Parliamentary Committee considering the second Chester & Holyhead Railway Bill, which included the bridges at Menai and Conwy. Stephenson outlined his proposal to erect two platforms each supported by three iron chains, to span the distance from the

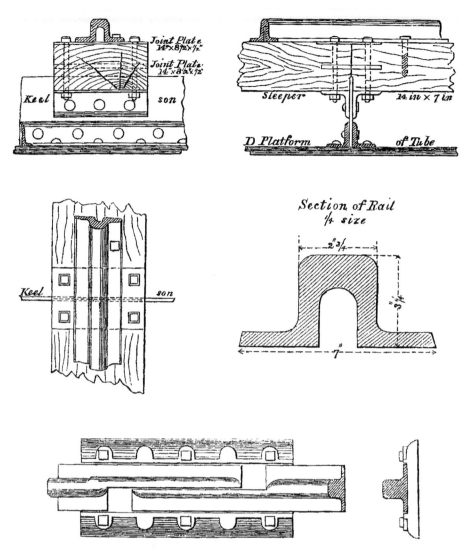

The permanent way used on the Britannia and Conwy Bridges consisted of bridge rails bolted to longitudinal timbers. This picture also shows the form of the expansion joints.

Britannia tower to the two land towers, a matter of 450ft. On these platforms he planned to build two pairs of elliptical tubes, one for each track, with an internal height of 25ft, and a width of 15ft. The tubes were to be fabricated from iron plates, riveted together and stiffened with angle irons. The top and bottom were to be of $\frac{7}{8}$in plates and the sides of $\frac{1}{2}$in material. An internal timber or iron frame would support the permanent way.

The weight of each tube was estimated at 450 tons. Drawings were prepared and calculations made by two assistants, George Berkeley and William P. Marshall – both destined to become distinguished engineers in later life. On the basis of these very elementary designs Stephenson considered that he had established the practicability of the concept. The committee was difficult to persuade.

When presenting his evidence Stephenson was asked if his calculations had been submitted to many other engineers. He replied that he had made them in conjunction with Mr Fairbairn of Manchester whose experience was greater than any man's in England. When further asked if the chains would form a permanent part of the finished bridge, his answer was non-committal but he thought it probable that they would be left as a prevention, though he had found that the tube itself would be quite sufficient to support any ordinary railway train. The proposal was supported by J.M. Rendel and by Maj.-Gen. Pasley RE, Chief Inspector of Railways for the Railway Commissioners. The Act received the Royal Assent at the end of June 1845.

Payment of Fairbairn's expenses was approved by the Chester & Holyhead directors, a sum of £3,000 being agreed. He was given a free hand to press ahead with his experiments entirely at his own discretion. Stephenson was content to leave the matter in Fairbairn's hands and managed only two short visits to the site while work was in progress. There was also a visit from several of the directors and the company secretary, George King. Otherwise Fairbairn was left to his own devices, Stephenson and his staff being fully occupied with planning and parliamentary work for some thirty-four railway schemes at home and others on the continent. The Railway Mania was already well under way.

For his own part, Fairbairn had a substantial business to run in Manchester, employing at its peak as many as 2,000 men. In between his frequent visits to Millwall much of the experimental work was supervised by his son Thomas, a partner in the business and manager of the shipyard. The reports on the first series of experiments in Clark's book were later compiled from Fairbairn's detailed notes, since Clark did not enter Stephenson's service until several months after the initial series of experiments had been satisfactorily completed. This inconvenient fact he glossed over in his book.

As the experiments progressed, Fairbairn realised that the work would call for an experienced assistant, with a deeper knowledge of mathematics than he possessed himself, and he sought permission from Stephenson to engage his old friend and fellow experimenter, Eaton Hodgkinson FRS (1789-1861). The aim was to use Hodgkinson's mathematical expertise to develop a general formula for assessing the strength of iron tubes. Hodgkinson had to delay a start until he had finished work already in hand and it was not until some days later that he was free to make a start at Millwall. As theory would suggest, it had very quickly became obvious that rectangular tubes were superior in strength although with all types the tops were generally the first parts to fail by buckling. Fairbairn was later criticised for wasting time on round and elliptical tubes but this was done at Stephenson's behest since he strongly favoured the elliptical shape.

It was then appreciated, apparently for the first time, that wrought iron lacked the great resistance to compression exhibited by cast iron. Not only was it found that the top of a girder required a greater cross-section of iron, but that the distribution of the metal was also critical. Formation of the top into a series of circular or rectangular cells was demonstrated to be the most effective solution. As early as 20 September 1845 Fairbairn had sent Stephenson a sketch of a tube, square cells top and bottom, almost exactly resembling those actually built, and this was some days before Hodgkinson had even started work at Millwall.

Three

The Millwall Experiments

Once Fairbairn received confirmation that the CHR Board had approved the expenditure on testing forms of iron tube to see which function most effectively as a bean, the work proceeded rapidly under the supervision of Thomas, Fairbairn's son and managing director of the shipyard, and his three senior foremen, Henry Ross, James Graham and Robert Murray. It would appear that Murray was closely involved also on the ship design side and responsible for the largest ship so far under construction, the *Pottinger* of 1,401 tons gross for the P&O Co., which was launched in 1846.

The shipyard on the Isle of Dogs was opened in 1835 in partnership with a former pupil, Andrew Murray, and was the second on the Thames to build exclusively in iron, being preceded by three years by Maudslay of Lambeth. The yard was never profitable in a highly competitive market as Fairbairn was not a man to cut corners. The business was finally brought to its knees by an Admiralty contract where the design was changed after all the iron plates had been ordered and were unsuitable for the amended design. Fairbairn's was not the first yard nor would it be the last to suffer from Admiralty patronage. Closure came in 1849 when the yard passed to John Scott Russell and in due course it became the birthplace of I.K. Brunel's behemoth, the *Great Eastern* steamship.

Fairbairn visited Millwall whenever the demands of his Manchester factory allowed, or could be left in the capable hands of his chief assistant, Mr Blair. Blair must have carried a great weight of responsibility for the smooth running of the Manchester works, yet surprisingly his invaluable services receive no recognition in Fairbairn's biography.

While tubular forms are common in nature because of their ability to resist forces equally from any direction, and their resistance to crushing is improved by internal diaphragms as in bamboo, the material of the walls is wastefully disposed when as in a beam, the loading comes from one direction only. But Stephenson was well aware of this and in his first proposal for an elliptical tube he increased the thickness of metal in the top and bottom. In his judgement the elliptical shape was deemed better, both to accommodate a train and to reduce the effects of wind pressure, though with its major dimension vertical it would appear inferior to a circular tube. Fairbairn thought otherwise.

It would be tedious to describe every experiment in detail, and it is only the final conclusion that affects the bridges. On 6 July 1845 the first circular tube was ready for testing. The ends were firmly supported on blocks, and a platform to hold weights was supported from the centre. Weights were added until the tube failed, generally by buckling of the top. After each failure the tube would be repaired, strengthened and retested. Tests were terminated when the bottom part of the tube failed, either by the metal tearing or the rivets shearing. A new tube of different shape or dimensions would then by put through the same process. The results of the tests were carefully recorded and later tabulated, and are reported in detail in Fairbairn's book on the tubular bridges. Later

Clark copied them for his own book though he took no part in the actual experiments. A full list of the tests is in the chronology on p.157.

On 19 July 1845 Stephenson was sent an invitation to visit the site at the end of the month to witness a final series of experiments on circular tubes. In his reply he reiterated his preference for the elliptical shape and again pressed for these to be tested. From the somewhat disappointing results on circular tubes, Fairbairn was reluctant to spend more time on curved tubes, and on 31 July he initiated a series of nine tests on rectangular tubes, which produced far more promising results. Under pressure from Stephenson the first test on an elliptical tube was carried out on 6 August, and witnessed by several of the directors accompanied by George King, the company secretary. Five more elliptical tubes were tested until 19 September, but again the results were disappointing. Stephenson was by no means convinced and as Samuel Smiles reported:

> *Mr Stephenson continued to hold that the elliptical tube was the right idea, and that sufficient justice had not been done to it. A year or two before his death Mr Stephenson remarked to the author that had the same arrangement for stiffening been adopted to which the oblong rectangular tubes owe a great part of their strength, a very different result would have been obtained.*

That was speculative, and there was a great pressure on Fairbairn to complete the tests, so to him it seemed pointless to devote more time and money to an inherently inferior concept. Since from the beginning there had been a clear understanding that any experiments were left entirely to his discretion he pressed ahead as he saw best. Fairbairn had established to his own satisfaction the superiority of rectangular tubes. Under pressure from the directors for more rapid progress, Stephenson accepted his defeat over the elliptical shape with apparent good grace though it may have rankled.

One incontrovertible fact arose from all the tests: wrought iron's tendency to buckle under pressure meant that it could not be stressed as heavily in compression as in tension. Some years before Eaton Hodgkinson, the Manchester mathematician and experimenter and a good friend of Fairbairn, had established that cast iron was roughly six times as strong in compression as in tension.

When compressed in a testing machine cylinders of cast iron would break up along shear planes roughly at forty-five degrees to the base. Similar tests on wrought iron would only result in plastic flow when the test piece was too short to buckle. This problem had not been recognised previously and was a discovery of fundamental importance where wrought iron would be used for structures in the future.

The Arrival of Eaton Hodgkinson

As the experiments proceeded the quantity of data accumulated, and Fairbairn was anxious to reach a general formula which could be applied to all forms of tubular beams. He suggested to Stephenson that Eaton Hodgkinson should be invited to assist. To this Stephenson readily agreed. Though Hodgkinson was a distinguished experimental scientist, his bias was towards academic investigations rather than towards the interests of a practising engineer. Much of his work proved most valuable though not always appreciated at the time. He had worked with Fairbairn before on the testing of iron, and their collaboration had proved fruitful. Later Hodgkinson was destined to become Professor of Mechanical Engineering at University College, London, where he probably found himself in more congenial surroundings.

At the time in question he was carrying out some investigations at the Blaenavon Ironworks in South Wales and was only able to make a flying visit to Millwall on 19 September 1845. By that date the majority of the initial tests were completed and he agreed to return to Millwall as soon as his business at Blaenavon had been brought to a close. Here there is a slight mystery, for no work had been done on cellular tops, and only the following day Fairbairn wrote to Stephenson proposing cellular construction in much the form it would later be used. Some time later Hodgkinson was to lay claim to the cellular concept and it is just possible that in the course of their discussions at Millwall, a seed had been sown, arising from earlier experiments which they had shared on the strength of columns.

Be that as it may, the breakthrough that would lead directly to the successful building of the first two tubular bridges came with Experiment XXIX made on 14 October 1845. This related to a rectangular tube, but the top plates were curved to form two parallel tubes resembling in cross section an old fashioned pair of spectacles. This tube eventually failed at the sides but the top was unharmed. An earlier series of experiments on iron columns under compression had shown that hollow circular tubes were the most effective, offering far greater resistance to buckling than solid columns of similar cross-sectional area. Fairbairn later expressed his opinion that:

> It is from this period we may date the disappearance of almost every difficulty respecting the construction of tubular and tubular girder bridges. The powerful resistance offered to compression by the cellular form of the top as exhibited in this experiment, at once decided in my mind the form to be adopted for the large tubes which now span the Conwy and Menai straits, and from this time forward I had no doubts as to the complete success of the undertaking.

The experiments were concluded on 14 October 1845, and Hodgkinson set about rationalising the data. For a few weeks little progress was made, and the directors of the CHR, under pressure from their shareholders, required Stephenson to submit a progress report for their half-yearly meeting on 11 February 1846. Three reports were submitted, one from Stephenson himself, and others from Fairbairn and Hodgkinson. Their very different tones are noticeable, reflecting their personal views.

A Progress Report to the Directors

Stephenson's own report, dated 9 February 1846, stated that his belief in the efficiency of a wrought iron tube had been vindicated by the results of the experiments. He conceded, albeit reluctantly, the superiority of a rectangular form of tube with extra metal in the top to resist compression. He recognised that the use of chains in the conventional manner would be totally unsuitable and stated that if, after further experiments, the use of chains could not be avoided, some new method of attachment must be devised to maintain the integrity of the tubes. In conclusion, he advised the directors that work on the masonry piers was scheduled to commence early in April.

Hodgkinson's report was mainly technical, but he was clearly unhappy with, as he saw it, the incompleteness of the experiments. He was by temperament very much a belt-and-braces man and concluded by saying: 'If it be determined to erect a bridge of tubes, I would beg to recommend that suspension chains be employed as an auxiliary…'

Fairbairn had no such qualms. After detailing his experiments, he came down firmly in favour of a rectangular tube with a cellular top, but recommended further experiments on a larger scale model. He stated his opinion that a tubular bridge could not only be constructed to carry railway traffic, but that:

In fact it should be a huge sheet-iron hollow girder, of sufficient strength and stiffness to sustain those weights; and provided that the parts are well-proportioned, and the plates properly riveted, you may strip off the chains, and leave it as a useful monument of the enterprise and the energy of the age in which it was constructed.

From the earliest discussions, Fairbairn had reacted instinctively against the use of suspension chains. He formalised his thinking in his book on the tubular bridges, remarking:

I always felt that in a combination of two bodies, the one of a perfectly rigid, and the other of a flexible nature, there was a principle of weakness; for the vibrations to which the one would be subjected would call into operation forces whose constant action upon the rivets and fastenings of the other could not but tend to loosen them and this by a slow but sure agency, to break up the bridge.

He never wavered from these views, while Stephenson, ever cautious when on uncertain ground, preferred to keep his options open. In any case, at that stage it was still considered that chains would be needed for the planned method of erecting the tubes and there was always the prospect that, if not required permanently, the redundant chains could then to be sold for use elsewhere.

Hodgkinson was becoming increasingly restless. He was a scientist and mathematician and out of sympathy with engineers whose sole interest was to rush ahead. Moreover, he had been sorely disappointed to find that he was regarded merely as a technical assistant rather than director of the experimental work. Now he feared that the engineers were heading into unknown territory, recklessly and without adequate data, due to commercial pressures, and he was by nature somewhat slow and pedantic in his own work. Fairbairn, on the other hand, never lacked confidence in his own abilities – far more so than Stephenson who suffered his moments of doubt. The pace at which the two engineers were prepared to push forward was remarkable by any standards, and seems almost incredible today. But Stephenson was anxious to placate the directors, who were becoming impatient under pressure from the shareholders who in their turn were complaining loudly of lack of progress and little prospect of dividends. To them, shareholder value was what it was all about. With no bridges there was no revenue and more importantly only renewed calls on their shares. Hodgkinson made clear his feelings in a letter to Stephenson early in March 1846, to the displeasure of Fairbairn who complained that Hodgkinson viewed the experiments as an abstract scientific investigation and was oblivious to time and money. To smooth things over, Stephenson agreed to Hodgkinson continuing his experimental work, leaving Fairbairn free to develop his ideas and to carry out tests on a scaled-down version of the actual tubes as proposed. Even at this early stage the overall dimensions of the full size tubes had been provisionally agreed in order to allow Francis Thompson, the architect, to proceed with final drawings for the foundations and towers.

The original £3,000 allocated for the experimental work had long been spent and as the costs continued to rise, Stephenson was criticised by the board for this unauthorised work. Fairbairn got wind of this, and thought he too was being held at fault for something over which he had no control. Stephenson wrote to Fairbairn explaining that it was he himself who the directors had in their sights and that it was a matter of no great moment. The total expenditure had risen to over £6,000, more than doubling the amount originally approved, and much of the extra had been spent on work doubtless of great scientific interest but of no practical benefit to the company. Stephenson could afford to ride out the storm for the directors needed him more than he did them, and Fairbairn was duly mollified.

The Model Tube

While the earlier experiments had provided important information regarding the top and bottom strength of a rectangular tube, little attention had been given to the sides. In 1846 and for some years thereafter there was no theoretical knowledge of the forces in the sides of a box beam or indeed in the web of other forms of beam. The general state of knowledge among practical engineers was exemplified by Stephenson's own comments to Samuel Smiles.

Mr Stephenson was also of the opinion that the sides of all trellis or lattice girders are useless, except for the purpose of connecting the top and bottom, and keeping them in their position. He told Smiles: 'I admit that there is no formula for valuing the solid tubes for strains, and that at the present we only ascribe to them the value or use of connecting the top and the bottom…'

Fairbairn had told Stephenson of his intention to construct a model tube exactly one-sixth of the dimensions of the finished tube in order to finalise the details and to establish the amount of metal required in the sides, though the latter had to be based largely on engineering judgement for lack of better information. The model tube was made 78ft in length with 75ft between the supports. The height was $4\frac{1}{2}$ft plus a layer of six 6in cells forming the top. The width was 2ft 8in. The first test took place on 10 July 1846 when the tube failed with a load of $35\frac{1}{2}$tons, due to the tearing away of the bottom plates, which in the beginning were made very thin.

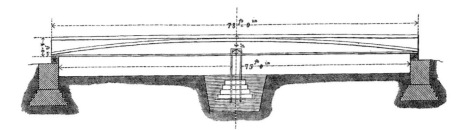

Above: Fairbairn's apparatus for testing the model tube.

Right: Model tube.

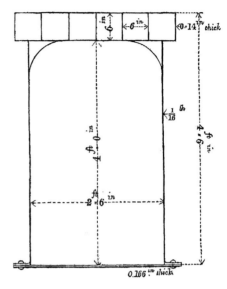

Throughout the series of tests which followed no alteration was made to the top cells but the bottom was strengthened until eventually the tube failed by buckling sideways. Internal diagonal stiffeners were then added together with external angle iron stiffeners on the sides. The final test came on 15 April 1846 when, with a load of $86\frac{1}{4}$ tons, a slight puckering was noticed in the top cells and the test was stopped. In this test the ratio of material in the top cells to the bottom plates was 12:11.

While these tests were under way, thought was given as to the best form for the cells in the full-sized tubes. In theory, there was much to be said for circular cells, but in practice, there would have been considerable practical difficulties in assembling these, particularly in obtaining access between the cells for painting, an important point often overlooked. For the full-sized tube a double layer of rectangular cells was first considered and later dismissed, again because of access problems. Earlier work on columns had shown that a rectangular box, re-inforced at the corners with angle irons, was a satisfactory substitute for a round cell, though using rather more material. The final decision was in favour of rectangular cells large enough to admit a man, and in a single row rather than the two first proposed.

It was at the board meeting in February 1846 that plans for the masonry were presented by Francis Thompson, the architect, and approved in order that tenders might be obtained to allow an early start. Even at this early stage, the overall dimensions of the tubes had been decided but, in fact, the circumstances offered little choice. The main spans had been fixed at 450ft clear – later amended to 460ft – which required the minimum height (or depth) of the tubes to be least 30ft. This gave a span/depth ratio in excess of 15:1, resulting in a very slim beam which is not usually apparent in photographs. The overall width was fixed at 15ft to allow sufficient internal width for the single line of traffic. On 17 March the contract drawings for the masonry were ready and no time was wasted for, on 14 April, the foundation stone was laid at Menai by Frank Forster, the resident engineer.

Meanwhile, Hodgkinson had been experimenting on wrought-iron box girders with cast-iron tops, and these he strongly advocated. Stephenson, however, accepted that it was too late for a major change to be acceptable, much to Fairbairn's relief. Stephenson himself had four box girder bridges constructed with cast-iron tops, and these will be described later. In principle the idea was sound enough but hardly applicable to the large tubes where the dead weight was critical. Scaling up from the model to a full-sized tube was far from a straightforward process, and advice was sought from one of the leading mathematicians of the day, George Biddell Airy (1801-1892), Astronomer-Royal. Despite his exalted position, he took much interest in solving practical engineering problems but he was not infallible. It was he who predicted that the Crystal Palace in its original form in Hyde Park would blow down (but a severe gale might have proved him right). However, his unequivocal opposition to the Atlantic telegraph cable on the grounds that it was 'mathematically impossible' was on a par with Robert Stephenson's declaration in Parliament and elsewhere that the Suez Canal too was an engineering impossibility. It was Airy who many years later advised Thomas Bouch somewhat ambiguously on wind forces on his planned crossing of the Forth and who gave evidence at the Tay Bridge Inquiry in 1880.

All that Airy could offer was a restatement of the square-cube law first put forward by Galileo (1564-1642), which stated that in the case of tubes, increasing the span to six times that of the model, and proportionately increasing the width and height, the weight was increased 6 x 6 x 6, or 216, times. This was correct in theory but not particularly helpful in practice. While the cross section of iron in the bottom and top chords could be calculated with the knowledge of the day, there was no basis of theory for estimating the strength of the sides and these could only be designed by scaling up from the sides of the model coupled with a high degree of engineering judgement on Fairbairn's part.

Whereas in wind tunnel tests or in naval architecture, models can provide vital information, their use in designing complex structures is hedged about with caveats. A former professor at Reading University, J.E. Gordon, who was closely involved with the aeronautical industry, wrote in his book on structures: 'The strength of any structure which is liable to fail because the material breaks cannot be predicted from models or by scaling up from previous experience.'

Such knowledge was unknown to Fairbairn and his contemporaries, and modelling techniques were used successfully in the nineteenth century until more sophisticated methods became available and structural engineering became a science rather than an art. The sides of the model had been found to require a certain amount of stiffening with angle irons to avoid buckling. In the full-sized tubes, the sides were formed of plates 2ft in width which were butt jointed. Instead of using flat cover plates, Fairbairn substituted tee irons back-to-back to provide the additional stiffness needed. The result was the weight of the sides alone was forty per cent of the total weight of each tube, divided equally between the plates and the tee irons. Fairbairn later agreed that they could have been lighter.

Ten years later, improved understanding of the sheer forces in the webs of girders, arising from Jourawski's pioneering work on Howe trusses carried out in Russia, would show that Fairbairn had been over-cautious in estimating the sides. Yet criticisms from Clapeyron and Jourawski himself, with the benefit of hindsight, do nothing to invalidate Fairbairn's achievement. The bridge had been built successfully and had already given a decade of good service. Over-generosity with iron was a small price to pay and the excess strength allowed the bridge to carry more traffic 120 years later that its builders could ever have imagined. Despite his carping, Clapeyron recognised the Britannia Bridge as being of 'originality and grandeur' which indeed it was while it lasted.

Clark went to great pains to calculate the breaking strength of the tubes. This was the criterion then employed rather than working to a maximum safe fibre stress which a few years later became commonplace. On 7 August 1846 Clark was instructed by Stephenson to write again to Professor Airy with a description of the final design of the Conwy tubes and to seek further information. Having described in some detail how he had arrived at the breaking weight, which he estimated to be 1,940 tons centrally placed, Clark went on to say:

> But, assuming the weight (of the tube) at 1,200 tons, it would then bear, in addition to its own weight, at the centre $1,940 - 600$ tons $= 1,340$ tons, or 2,680 tons distributed throughout, which, allowing a ton per foot for trains, is nearly seven times as much as can be required for practical purposes.

This method of calculating a 'factor of safety' was widely used and appeared to give very satisfactory results, or so Clark and Stephenson thought. Airy, however, was of a rather different opinion, and wrote back to explain that the correct calculation would be, using distributed loads: 3,880 tons divided by $(1,200 + 400$ tons$)$ = a factor of safety of 2.42. A similar calculation for the Britannia tubes treated as simple beams gave a factor of 2.52. In years to come, a factor of 4 became the norm for wrought iron structures and 6 for cast iron. Stephenson was not dismayed and would have no truck with such newfangled ideas. His views were expressed by Clark:

> But as the weight of the bridge is a permanent and unvariable strain, whereas the load to which the bridge may be subjected in use is the only variable load which has to be considered, it appeared to Mr Stephenson that when the weight of the structure formed so very important a part of the whole strain, he was justified in making the assumption as above, and retaining the usual factor itself.

Approached from another point of view, as Clark was wont to do (though not on this occasion), taking the maximum tensile strength of wrought iron as, conservatively, 18 tons per square inch, a factor of safety of 2.42 would give a maximum fibre stress under full load of 7.4 tons per square inch. Fairbairn's experimental tests on fatigue in wrought iron reported in 1860 showed that repetitive stresses exceeding 7 tons per square inch were dangerous and led to early failure from fatigue. This confirmed earlier work by James and Galton reported in 1849, when a maximum working load of one third of the breaking load had been recommended. Unknowingly, Clark and Stephenson were sailing very close to the wind. Derrick Beckett's calculations for the Conwy tubes, using modern mathematics, show a comparable stress of 7.35 tons per square inch. It was fortunate that for many years afterwards the weight of trains did not approach the maximum level, and that by the time they did remedial measures had already been undertaken.

The Tube Design is Finalised by Fairbairn

The design work on the tubes went ahead fast in Fairbairn's drawing office in Manchester. Apart from slight variations in plate thickness, the design was repetitive along the length of each tube. Particular care was taken that cover plates provided full strength at each joint and that all joints were staggered to avoid lines of weakness. The bottom chord was formed from six cells with two thicknesses of plates above and below which were slightly thicker towards mid-span. Each cell was 28in by 21in. The eight top cells were similar but 21in square. The sides were of a single thickness of plate, 24in wide, with all vertical joints butted and with tee irons riveted back-to-back. In this case, the plates were increased in thickness towards the abutments. Rivets were spaced 4in horizontally and 3in vertically and varied in size from $\frac{15}{16}$in to $1\frac{1}{8}$in. In all at Britannia some two million rivets were driven.

In July 1846, Mr Blair, Fairbairn's personal assistant and chief draughtsman, was able to report completion of the working drawings for the tubes and by 29 July tenders had been accepted for 8,000 tons of iron, orders going out early in August for delivery in 1847. Of all the unsung heroes of the tubular bridges, Blair must rank among the most important for his contribution behind the scenes, coupled with exemplary patience in dealing with Clark. The latter, having played no part in the original 1845 series of experiments, had closely watched the work on the model tube, and had reported every move back to Stephenson. So much knowledge had he acquired since starting in Stephenson's office in April 1846 that after three months he was sent up to Manchester to keep an eye on developments there. He claims:

> In order to obtain Mr Fairbairn's practical assistance in elaborating the detail, the author was directed by Mr Stephenson to proceed to Manchester and, in conjunction with that gentleman, to complete the drawings for the bottom and sides of the Conwy Bridge... He was assisted by Mr Blair, by whom, under his immediate inspection and directions, the first drawings for the tubes were executed; and the general dimensions, thickness of the plates and all important details involving any theoretical principles, were thus determined.

Clark was no fool nor, by any standard, was he a genius, and it is his ridiculous claims of this kind that undermine the authority of parts of his book which in other respects is a valuable historical record. Moreover, William Pole's contribution to Clark's book on strength of materials was the first source of such material generally available to engineers, and would be regarded as a standard work for years to come. Little more need be said on this subject and readers can only form their own conclusions as to whom credit was due.

Four

The Remarkable Rise of Edwin Clark

A new star was to arise in the firmament in March 1846. The unexpected appearance in Stephenson's office of a young man of thirty-two, Edwin Clark by name, came as a complete surprise to all, not least to Stephenson himself. Clark had turned up unannounced at Great George Street, bearing only a letter of introduction from an unnamed friend in Birmingham. Though the Railway Mania of 1845-1846 was already under way and the office extremely busy, Clark managed to attract the attention of John Sanderson, Stephenson's chief clerk, brother-in-law and personal friend. Sanderson was sufficiently impressed to procure an interview with 'The Chief', as Stephenson was known by all his staff.

Edwin Clark was the eldest of three sons of a prosperous Buckingham hand lace manufacturer but, with the introduction of machinery, the Clarks and their lace makers fell on hard times. Fortunately for young Edwin he had received a sound education, including three years in France, and at the age of sixteen he was placed for two years with his uncle, a London solicitor. The law not proving to his taste, Clark turned to self-education, with a particular interest in scientific matters. During this time he seems to have sown a few wild oats and, perhaps unjustly, gained the reputation of a ne'er-do-well. With the wolf never far from the door he became in turn an assistant to a surgeon, unsuccessfully applied for a place in the Excise and finally resorted to teaching at his old school.

Despite his financial problems, Clark managed to obtain a place at Cambridge in 1834 to read classics but this not proving agreeable he devoted a further eighteen months to the study of mathematics, though leaving college for whatever reason without taking his degree. His explanation was lack of money. Thinking to make a career as a railway surveyor at a time when their services were at a premium, he was persuaded to try his luck with Stephenson. The rest, as they say, is history!

There are only Clark's accounts to record his early days at 24 Great George Street. He was undoubtedly a presentable young man with a lively intelligence, a useful ability at fairly basic mathematics and a persuasive tongue. His meteoric rise in civil engineering without any previous background must have astonished and dismayed his contemporaries, Stephenson's old and trusted lieutenants. His first meeting with 'The Chief' was recorded in a letter to a friend: 'I have had a very pleasant and satisfactory interview with Mr Stephenson. He treated me most kindly and promised to do something or anything for me.'

In a later letter he reports:

> *I have got put into my hands by Mr Robert Stephenson all his ideas and wishes about the intended bridge, by far the greatest work ever attempted by mortals... All is at present in*

embryo. I am sole manager of the plans and sole calculator of all the mathematical work and have liberty to perform any experiments… I got the appointment by his own examination of me, not by mere introduction, which gives me greater hopes of success; but I am not sanguine.

I have made a model of the bridge for Mr Stephenson and we spend every day two or three hours chatting on the subject. He is a delightful fellow and a very clever practical man.

No one has seen fit to publish a biography of Edwin Clark and most of what is known of his activities is from his own reports in the book he wrote on Stephenson's instructions. There is no doubt that he made himself useful, especially after Fairbairn's resignation, but many of his claims are suspect.

It is clear that Stephenson's thoughts were concentrated on the Britannia Bridge, by far the larger undertaking of the two, beside which the Conwy Bridge seemed of less importance. In fact this was far from the case for the 400ft span at Conwy was itself a leap into the unknown and without its successful completion the erection of the larger spans at Menai could not have been undertaken so successfully.

With Clark's appointment, Fairbairn found that his experiments on the model tube would be much more closely observed than hitherto. The crucial series of tests on various shapes of tube were made at Millwall between July and October 1845 and had been carried out under the supervision of Fairbairn and his son. At an advanced stage, after the rectangular top cells had been proposed, they were joined by Eaton Hodgkinson, the mathematician. Although Stephenson had been sent frequent progress reports, his many commitments meant that he could only spare time for two short visits while the experiments were under way. These fundamental experiments were completed months before Clark made his appearance. After his appointment Clark's function was to closely observe, record and report back work on the model tube to Stephenson over Fairbairn's head. There was a spy in the camp or so it must have seemed!

Nonetheless, Fairbairn appreciated Clark's diligence and enthusiasm despite his lack of practical experience and commented on this in his book, finishing: '…he attained a degree of expertness highly creditable to the talents of a gentleman whose previous knowledge of practical mechanics was not extensive.'

In fairness to Clark, it must be said that if he was somewhat wet behind the ears when he started in April 1846 he had learned fast in the two years up to Fairbairn's resignation, after which he carried a heavy responsibility as resident engineer for the ironwork. He was not alone, however, for his brother, Joshua Latimer Clark, eight years his junior, was to prove a capable assistant. The resident engineer for bridges and stations, Charles Heard Wild, was available to offer valuable assistance from his own more extensive experience. Not least the veterans, Frank Forster and Alexander Ross were on hand when needed. The ironwork contractors too proved themselves both competent and efficient and deserving of much credit. Finally, mention should be made of John McLaren, the inspector of ironwork, who bore a heavy supervisory burden and his assistant, Charles Rolfe.

A Sad Lapse at Brotherton

Although not in strict chronological sequence, this is an appropriate point to tell the story of Clark's personal venture into tubular bridge design. Having, as he claimed, designed the Conwy and Britannia tubes, the smaller bridge at Brotherton should not have taxed his powers too much, but a remarkable structure it turned out to be.

With the completion of the tubular bridges, the Clark brothers would move on to other things and Edwin was commissioned by Stephenson to design a tubular bridge over the River Aire at Brotherton, on the York & North Midland Railway. This was not an unqualified success and proved an embarrassment to Stephenson at a time when he was planning to cut his workload and enjoy the pleasure of his yacht. However, with the completion of the Welsh bridges and under Stephenson's patronage, Clark was eased into a new appointment as his obituarist explains:

> When the Bridges were approaching completion, an opening occurred for an engineer to this great undertaking [the Electric & International Telegraph Co.] and although Mr Clark had hitherto no experience whatever in electrical work, yet Robert Stephenson, having now had many years' acquaintance with him, unhesitatingly recommended him to the post and in August, 1850, he was appointed, accordingly, Engineer-in-Chief to the Company, a position he held for many years.

George Parker Bidder, Stephenson's close friend, had played a leading part in the early development of the electric telegraph and was a Director of the Electric Telegraph Co. from its inception. Clark's appointment was a neat exercise in cronyism in an age when it thrived. Latimer was carried along on his brother's coat tails and became his assistant once again, only to succeed him as chief engineer some years later. Edwin went on to develop an extensive practice as a consulting engineer, mainly abroad, and also, we are told, took up contracting on a large scale. He lived to the age of eighty, but his later exploits never attracted the same attention as did the tubular bridges, not was he destined to find a place in the Pantheon of great engineers.

The bridge at Brotherton was the smallest and most controversial, though the least known, of the British train-sized tubular bridges. There the York & North Midland branch between Burton Salmon and Knottingley crosses the River Aire. The YNMR was one of George Hudson's projects, engineered by George and Robert Stephenson, and with John Cass Birkinshaw (1811-1867), Robert Stephenson's first articled pupil, as resident engineer on the Knottingley branch. Hudson's earlier scheming had produced a through route to York from Euston. Now his devious mind envisaged an alternative route to York from Kings Cross by linking up with the Great Northern which had reached Knottingley from the south. As a result, the GNR traffic became more important to the YNMR than its own, since the bridge at Brotherton completed a vital link in what was to become the East Coast Route to Scotland.

After initial arguments with the Aire & Calder Navigation about obstructing the channel with the piers required for an arched bridge, Stephenson resorted to a tubular bridge spanning from bank to bank to which the canal company would be hard put to offer any objections, try though they might. The ironwork was manufactured in the Stephenson locomotive works at Newcastle, from where it was delivered in prefabricated sections for final erection on temporary scaffolding designed not to obstruct the passage of canal traffic. Contractors for the whole branch including erection of the bridge were Hutchinson & Ritson.

The design of the bridge is attributed to Edwin Clark in his official obituary, and having a free hand after experience gained at the Welsh bridges, Clark ventured to omit the cells in the top chord altogether. Since the first tube passed the load tests to the satisfaction of Capt. Wynne RE, it undoubtedly paved the way for the adoption of this simplified construction several years later at Montréal where all spans barring the centre were of 242ft. The twin tubes at Brotherton were 237ft overall, spanning 232ft clear, and 20ft high at the eaves. Where they differed to a remarkable extent from the other tubular bridges was in cross section, being a bare 10ft 3in internally at the base and a foot less at the top. Just what possessed Clark to impose such a restriction on the size of rolling stock that could pass through the bridge is impossible to guess other than false economy, since the YNMR was a company that did not throw its money around and had probably not envisaged the effects of Hudson's machinations.

The first tube was passed by Capt. Wynne on 2 July 1851 without any adverse comment. He appears to have been one of the more easygoing inspectors, but in this instance he was to find himself with much explaining to do and for good reason. For a few weeks all seemed well and work was well under way on the second tube. On 17 September, the general manager of the Great Northern issued a report to the effect that, due to the restricted width of the tube, carriage lamps had been knocked off and a passenger had injured his hand. Even more seriously he reported that the latest GNR brake vans had only half an inch clearance either side over the lamp irons, even when not in motion, and could not be used on what had now become the Great Northern's main line to York.

Naturally, the YNMR referred the matter to Robert Stephenson as the engineer accountable. He replied at some length that clearances on other railways were similar if not worse, and that the GNR was at fault in introducing such wide rolling stock. He recommended that bars should be fitted on the carriage windows. As Stephenson was about to go abroad he delegated the matter to George Berkeley, by then a senior assistant, who conveyed this information to the GNR. They promptly forwarded the letter to the Railway Department of the Board of Trade, declining all responsibility, bearing in mind that the first tube had been approved and was in daily use.

Captain Wynne Objects

After inspecting progress on the almost completed second tube in November 1851, Capt. Wynne warned that he would not pass it for traffic, explaining somewhat lamely that when inspecting the first tube back in July his mind had been concentrated on matters of strength. He knew and the company knew that at this stage he had no power to close the first tube. A month later the YNMR advised the Railway Department that it wished to open the second tube, and that Stephenson would be consulted as soon as he returned to

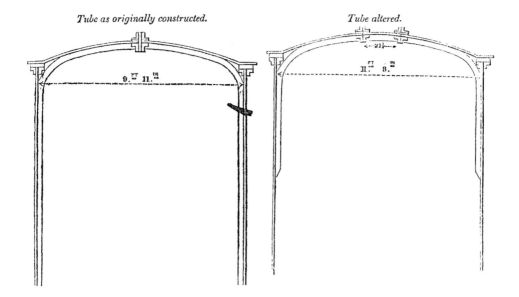

Tube as originally constructed.

Tube altered.

Above: The tubes at Brotherton as originally built and after widening to meet the demands of the Board of Trade.

Right: A more detailed section of Edwin Clark's original design for the tubes at Brotherton – note the use of bridge rails as at Britannia.

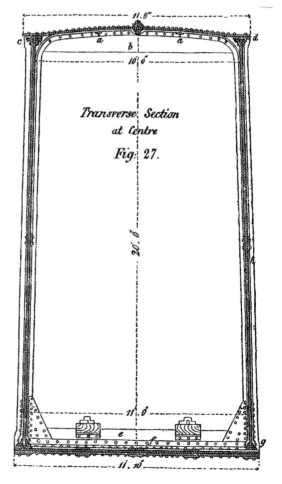

Transverse Section at Centre

Fig. 27.

An early photograph of the Brotherton Tubular Bridge over the River Aire, probably taken by the Calotype process on a paper negative.

A later view looking through the Brotherton tubes. The additional section inserted in the top to widen the tube is clearly visible.

England. Each month the YNMR requested an inspection and each time Capt. Wynne reported unfavourably. The Board of Trade was driven to complain, as well they might, that the repetition of inspections by their officers was 'productive of inconvenience'. At the end of June 1852 Wynne yet again inspected the tube and once more refused to pass it for passenger traffic. Tempers were beginning to fray.

Stephenson, who had been wintering in Egypt and cruising the Nile on his private yacht, had returned from abroad in May, and by July he had submitted a scheme for widening the tube, though he continued to argue that it was adequate as it stood and pointed out that there had been no accidents to date. Capt. Wynne, standing firm, wrote in his report of 3 July 1852:

> *I will instance a somewhat analguous* [sic] *case, where there has not been that immunity from danger. I refer to certain bridges of a peculiar construction that existed some time ago on the Manchester & Bolton Railway.*

The Manchester & Bolton was efficiently engineered by Jesse Hartley (1780-1860), with structures in the best canal-building tradition. Hartley is perhaps better known for his superb docks at Liverpool. The greater part of the line was laid out for three tracks, two for passengers and one for goods, but in the event only two were ever laid. Several over-bridges were built spanning the three tracks, but with a row of cast-iron pillars between each track, leaving a clear opening of barely 10ft. Since the carriages were 6ft 4in wide clearances were tight. In those halcyon days before safety legislation, railway servants were treated as expendable, and there seems to have been little concern shown at accidental deaths. Even after the passing of the Regulation of Railways Act of 1840, conditions only slowly improved and many an accident went unreported where it could be hushed up.

Quoting from an 1846 report by Capt. Coddington RE, Wynne says:

> *The guard, whose business it is to keep a look out on all sides, has only 15 inches between the side of his break* [sic] *and these columns, and does his duty at the risk of his life; in fact I find that on 26 July 1844 a guard was killed by striking against one of them and in November 1842 another guard was killed…*

In fact, he had been found lying dead on the track and the bridge was blamed. Capt. Wynne goes on to say that subsequently another fatal accident occurred at one of these bridges and that they had been removed and replaced by others. Clark's error of judgement had left Stephenson in an indefensible position. Moreover, the YNM's own open third carriages were 6in wider than those on the Manchester & Leeds, a fact which must have been known to Clark. It was for very sound reasons that the dangers of leaning out were traditionally emphasised.

A deadlock seemed to have been reached until an aristocratic intervention by the Duke of Montrose, whose complaint to Lord Colchester, Vice-President of the Board of Trade, swiftly brought matters to a head and it was agreed that the two companies should share the cost of effecting a widening, with Stephenson's firm contributing £500. The roof of each tube was split down the centre line, the sides forced apart, and a plate 21½in wide inserted in the gap. This, claimed Stephenson with satisfaction, made the bridge even stronger than before. Maybe, but the cutting away of the side angle stiffeners to give an additional 6in of clearance internally would have weakened the sides considerably. On 11 October, the second tube was opened and the first then closed for alteration, reopening on 16 November. The cost was £1,283 and, in a fit of unwonted generosity, Robert Stephenson & Co. paid half. It had been an embarrassing affair for all concerned and little credit to Stephenson himself, though much of the time he was far away and putting his trust in Clark.

By 1898, the bridge was showing signs of deterioration and in common with many other early bridges of doubtful strength the time had come for its replacement. In 1901 tenders were sought for a new steel truss bridge. At the end of 1903, the new bridge had been completed by the Cleveland Bridge & Engineering Co. at a cost of £20,224. For all its limitations the first bridge had given fifty years' service on a busy main line. Stephenson frequently cited it as an example of the superiority of a tubular bridge, comparing it favourably with the Warren girder bridge over Newark Dyke, also on the GNR main line and opened the same year as Brotherton. Stephenson did have a point, for the Newark Bridge was very slim and its pin joints were subject to wear and became noisy with time. But those were teething troubles with a radically new design, which today is more popular than ever before. Brotherton as originally built is almost forgotten, an early experiment which failed.

Five

The Architect and the Troubleshooter

To those familiar with the story of the great tubular bridges both in Wales and in Canada the name of Francis Thompson should be familiar, yet little has been written about the man who may justifiably be described as being among the greatest of the railway architects. There were many who contributed to our heritage of fine railway buildings, but strangely their work has attracted few chroniclers while there is a superabundance of literature on other aspects of railway construction. Yet it is fair to say that the works of architects have, despite the vandalism at Euston and elsewhere, long outlived most of those of even the greatest of the early engineers.

Of the many talented architects who contributed to the railway scene, some like John Dobson designed only one great station where at Newcastle Central, unusually, he also engineered the magnificent wrought iron train shed. Mostly this latter duty fell to engineers who, in early days, contented themselves with simple industrial pattern pitched roofs of the type devised by Charles Fox for use at Euston and Curzon Street, Birmingham, followed some years later by Charles H. Wild at Chester.

On the other hand, Sir William Tite MP (1798-1873), who perhaps had the most extensive railway practice of all, basked in the limelight of popular approbation and stood for public office, while at the same time pursuing extensive commercial interests. Such a

A view of the Britannia Bridge looking south from Telford's bridge. The unusually slim nature of the tubes is apparent and the whole structure has a more elegant appearance than it is given credit for.

life would have been out of character for Francis Thompson and this may explain why so much of his career has remained obscure until recently.

Thompson's biographer, the late Oliver F. Carter FRIBA, once surmised that his collaboration with Stephenson and Fairbairn in the design of the Britannia Bridge was: 'Perhaps one of the best examples of the engineer and architect working successfully together to be found in the early Victorian age.'

Francis Thompson (1808–1895) was the son of a Suffolk county surveyor and in 1830, at the age of twenty-two, he first sought his fortune in Canada. His destination was Montréal, where the rapidly developing city already had a population of 30,000. There, in association with another Norfolk man, John Wells, he designed houses and commercial buildings. From 1834, in partnership with H.B. Parry, he also took on commissions for public buildings. Civil unrest in 1837 caused Thompson to dissolve his partnership and return to England, where he made the acquaintance of George and Robert Stephenson. Employment soon followed on the North Midland Railway, engineered by the two Stephensons, and the line, authorised in July 1836, opened in May 1840. Thompson seems to have been left much to his own devices while maintaining a 'house style'. Apart from two major stations at Derby and Leeds, there were twenty-four others

Britannia Bridge, the Caernarfon Tower almost completed. This is a remarkable Calotype photograph taken by an unknown photographer on 13 September 1849, showing that work on the two short land spans is well advanced. (3S/1950)

One of the great stone lions in its original majesty. Today the lions are overshadowed by the road deck above. (Photo by Eric de Maré. Crown Copyright. Royal Commission on the Ancient and Historical Monuments of Wales.)

– all different. It was here that Thompson first became acquainted with the up-and-coming railway engineer Alexander McKenzie Ross.

The tubular bridges offered an enormous challenge, for visually they were dominated by the stark simplicity of the great iron tubes, however tastefully they might be painted to blend in. Nevertheless, most views of the Britannia tubes are taken from the shore nearby and give a false impression of this bulk. When seen from Telford's bridge, the tubes are slim and almost delicate, and the bridge as a whole looks far less dominant and far more graceful. At Conwy the tubes were in direct contrast to their close neighbours, Telford's road suspension bridge and the ancient castle. In deference to the adjoining Conwy Castle, Telford had chosen castellated towers, and Thompson was left with little choice but to follow, despite the visual disparity of the uncompromising lines of the tubes and the graceful parabola of Telford's chains alongside.

Nor was the position improved by the rise in the roof of the tubes to the central point, though the engineering reasons for this were impeccable. Material was saved, and the reduction in dead weight allowed an increased working load. There was also a worthwhile saving in cost with no loss of strength. This was achieved only at the price of an aesthetic loss. At Britannia the circumstances were vastly different and the roof line rose on a barely perceptible parabolic curve to a peak at the Britannia tower. Although at Conwy Thompson had done his best, there were as always, critics, including a correspondent to *The Builder* who proclaimed that: 'Its unmitigated ugliness is much to be deplored.'

There had been proposals to improve the Conwy Bridge with appropriately medieval trimmings so dear to the Victorian heart, such as cast-iron machicolations and loopholes. Fortunately, the chronically impecunious state of the Chester & Holyhead Co. ruled out these delights to the eye. In the same spirit, there were proposals for the Britannia tower at Menai to be crowned with a great statue of Britannia herself, but once again fate intervened in an economy where boom and bust followed in quick succession. Money was scarce and the lady vanished without a trace.

It was at Menai that Thompson's powers were really put to the test. At a board meeting of the CHR in January 1846, Thompson was briefed to prepare drawings for the next meeting of the Board on 11 February. Due to the urgency of the matter, Thompson had very little to go on. The height and width of the tubes had been established and the required spans between the towers and abutments were known. Provision had to be made for the suspension chains, although whether or not they would remain permanently was still undecided. It must be assumed that the preliminary sketches had Stephenson's approval, for they were submitted to the board at the February meeting, where they were approved and instructions issued to go out to tender.

Contract drawings were sent out forthwith and by 25 March the tenders were in. Six contractors were involved and three master masons, John Hemingway, Benjamin Nowell and Charles Pearson, acting as a consortium, were awarded the Britannia contract for £130,000. On 10 April Frank Forster, resident engineer at Menai, laid the foundation stone. Things moved fast in 1846!

Frank Forster (1800–1852) started his career, as did so many early railway engineers, as a colliery viewer or manager. In 1830 he turned to railway building and joined

The lions.

Robert Stephenson's staff on the London & Birmingham Railway. There he quickly gained the confidence of his young chief, and afforded him valuable assistance in seeing the Bill through Parliament and subsequently in building the line. In the course of their work, they became close personal friends and Forster was made resident engineer for the Kilsby Tunnel, the source of so many seemingly intractable problems. Following the completion of the Britannia Bridge and the Chester to Holyhead line, he returned to coal mining, which he proclaimed to be his favourite pursuit, with consultancy work in America.

Around this period, the sanitation of London had reached such an appalling state that the authorities were forced very reluctantly into taking action and the Metropolitan Commission of Sewers was formed to tackle the scandalous situation. Frank Forster was unanimously appointed as chief engineer. What a poisoned chalice it was to prove! Demanding though the engineering challenge would be, the internal politics drove him to distraction. To quote the words of his obituary:

> *This is not a place to detail the prejudices that had to be encountered, the contending interests to be conciliated, the acrimony to be submitted to, the interferences to be put up with, and even the slanders to be refuted… A little more kindliness out of doors, and a more general and hearty support from the Board he served, might have prolonged a valuable life, which as it was, became embittered and shortened by the labours, thwartings and anxieties of a thankless office. Worn out by annoyances Mr Forster resigned his appoint-ment and died a few weeks afterwards in his fifty-second year.*

But at Menai the challenge was of an altogether different order. Forster was answerable to only one master who commanded his unquestioning loyalty and he rose to meet it with outstanding success.

Faced with the need to provide three towers and chain anchorages at the abutments, Thompson was left with a limited choice of styles to adopt. At Derby he had only three companies to satisfy. At Chester, where there were four, an Italianate style proved an acceptable compromise between often-warring factions. At Menai there was but the one master and the choice of a design associated with ancient Egyptian temple pylons was proposed and accepted. The massive solidity of the towers was complementary to the strictly utilitarian form of the tubes, where form followed function unchallenged. As a sop to those who demanded decoration, Grecian motifs were sparingly applied to the three towers. It is interesting to speculate what horrors might have arisen had Thompson fallen victim to the Gothic Revival, then in full swing.

Thompson was not out of step with the times, for the Egyptian Revival had been in vogue for some years and it was to reach its zenith in the Egyptian Courts at the Great Exhibition of 1851 where it was encouraged by the architect Owen Jones, Superintendent of the Exhibition. Even the great stone lions, crouched on their plinths, two at each portal of the Britannia Bridge, displayed Egyptian ancestry and were described by Sir Francis Head: 'These noble animals, which are of the antique, knocker-nosed, pimple-faced Egyptian instead of the real Numidian form, although sitting, are 12ft high, 25ft long and weigh 30 tons.'

These handsome beasts were sculpted by John Thomas, sculptor and architectural draughtsman, who had been commissioned to carry out much decorative work on the newly risen Palace of Westminster. Unlike Britannia on her tower, the lions escaped the financial purges and contributed much to the character of the finished work. Today they remain in all their pride, but deep in the shadow of the new road deck above.

The central Britannia tower is 60ft by 50ft 5in at its base, firmly resting on the Britannia rock, and it rises 221ft 3in. The land towers are 18ft lower. The hollow walls average about 10ft in thickness, with a cladding of Anglesey Penmon limestone hiding the softer Runcorn sandstone used for the interior of rubble masonry in mortar. All material was brought in by sea and stone for the Britannia tower was hoisted directly from the holds of the vessels. Altogether 2,177 loads were delivered.

In the original design no provision was made for lifting the tubes, which Stephenson had proposed at the beginning should be built on scaffolding erected between the abutments and the land towers. The completed tubes were to be rolled out over a platform suspended on chains until they met at the central tower. To maintain the platform level at all times, wagons loaded with pig iron would be placed on the platform and withdrawn as the tube advanced. Admirable in theory, the practicalities do not seem to have been worked out in detail, and certainly not at the time that Thompson produced his contract drawings. Since the platforms would each have required four chains, according to Clark, these would have had to be attached to the roof of each finished tube but divided at the abutments to allow the passage of trains. Fortunately, as Clark tells us in his book, he came forward with a proposal which offered a better solution. He reports that while waiting for a train at Crewe on 14 July 1846 he had observed an erection gang raising a cast-iron water tank with screw jacks. From this sprang his suggestion to build the tubes on land, float them out, and raise them using hydraulic jacks, or presses as they were then generally known.

Having previously given the matter much thought, particularly as to how the chains should be attached to the tubes, Fairbairn was driven to the conclusion that such auxiliary support was not only impractical but positively dangerous. He informed Stephenson of this grave concern on 18 July, urging him to reach a decision. At first Stephenson was not enthusiastic. Having made his mind up to a certain course of action he was, as usual, loathe to change it. Fairbairn could see the advantages and eventually he and Clark prevailed on Stephenson to recognise the merits of the new method. Stephenson replied two days later to the effect that he did not oppose the scheme in principle, if it could be achieved safely. Moreover, the estimated saving was too great to be taken lightly. He pressed Fairbairn and Clark to visit him in London if necessary as he was under great pressure with three Bills going through the Lords. Not least there would be a great saving in the cost of chains, estimated at £150,000. While, from their earliest discussions, Fairbairn had ventured the opinion that auxiliary support for the finished tubes was unnecessary, this was a point which he repeated in his report to the Board in February 1846. Once it was finally established that chains would not be needed during erection, they were abandoned.

Clark's first suggestion of building up the towers under the tubes as they were raised was quickly dropped, since the work was already well in hand on the foundations, while the first tube would not be ready for many months, causing an intolerable delay. The chosen solution was to leave recesses 6ft deep in the towers to accommodate the ends of the tubes, and to corbel out the bottom of the land towers to allow the ends of the tubes to be slotted into the Britannia tower and then swung sideways into position at the land ends. Thompson was called on to modify his design so that work could go ahead without further delay.

At Conwy, Thompson's task was very much simpler, for in the absence of any demands for navigational access the tubes needed to be raised only 24ft above high water. The bridge abutments were excluded from the original contract No.6 for two miles of line on either side of the river. This was awarded to John Evans of Oldham in August 1845, despite Stephenson's preference for one major contract for the whole line. In fact only one such tender was received from Edward Ladd Betts, who appears again later as part of that other 'great triumvirate', Peto, Brassey & Betts, projectors and main contractors for the Grand Trunk Railway of Canada, and many other ventures.

John Evans was not to enjoy his success for he died within weeks and the contract was reassigned to his son, William Evans of Cambridge. Even before the second Act had received the Royal Assent there was a call for tenders for constructing the Conwy Bridge approaches and abutments. Again, William Evans was successful with a tender of £26,500 accepted on 6 May 1846. Only six days later the foundation stone was laid by Alexander Ross, the resident engineer. The paths of Thompson and Ross had crossed again, as they were to do once more in Canada. Evans was to prove an exceptionally competent and enterprising contractor when, as will be seen later, he not only became general contractor for the whole of the works at Conwy but later was appointed a senior manager of the Canada Works in Birkenhead which supplied all the rolling stock and iron bridges for the Grand Trunk Railway of Canada – including the Victoria Tubular Bridge and many others.

By this time, Thompson's work on the tubular bridges was almost complete, and he could safely leave them in the experienced and capable hands of Forster and Ross. There were some twenty-four stations of varying size to be designed and built, from the extensive Italianate structure at Chester, a counterpart in size to the late Georgian station at Derby, down to small wayside stations. The resident engineer for bridges and stations was Charles Heard Wild, a young engineer who had proved himself to a draughtsman of exceptional ability when he started work under George Watson Buck on the Manchester & Crewe line. Assisting Wild was George Grove who, after a spell under Clark at Britannia, forsook engineering to become a distinguished musicologist and compiler of *Grove's Dictionary of Music*. Wild will reappear later when he went to work for Stephenson on the Cairo & Alexandria Railway, but in the interim he would play an important part in the story of the Crystal Palace of 1851 and its later development at Sydenham. Both Thompson and Ross will be met later when the Victoria Bridge at Montréal and the Grand Trunk Railway are considered.

Captain Moorsom: a Steady Hand on the Tiller

One of the unsung heroes of the Chester & Holyhead Railway was Capt. Constantine Richard Moorsom (1792-1861). Moorsom was essentially a man of affairs with extensive maritime experience rather than an engineer, and it was in this capacity that he served the CHR so well, acting as a troubleshooter on many occasions.

The company was very much London-based, with offices in the City in Moorgate, and half the directors, including Moorsom himself, were also on the Board of the London & Birmingham Railway, later to become the core of the mighty London & North Western Railway. This financially powerful organisation was to rescue the impecunious CHR more than once and eventually swallowed it up in 1859.

Few of the CHR directors had the time, much less the inclination, to venture into what they regarded as the wilds of North Wales and Moorsom was offered, and accepted, the appointment of resident director on a salary of £1,000 per annum, together with the use of a house, Gorphwysfa, with twenty-six acres of land, where he lived rent-free and in some style. The house was on rising ground overlooking the Strait and close to Telford's Bridge. Apart from two entrance lodges, it had extensive outbuildings and a large greenhouse. Unfortunately, the completed railway line passed only a few yards from the front windows, and it was probably for this reason that the company had been obliged to acquire it. With the completion of the railway, Sir Joseph Paxton came into the picture with grand plans for a 500-bed hotel on the land. Although a start was made, funds soon ran out, and eventually the land was sold off in 1861.

At the London end, day-to-day matters were in the hands of George King, the company secretary. This was far from a mere administrative post, involving responsibility for technical decisions also. Robert Stephenson, the company engineer, was based in Westminster at his offices in Great George Street and due to his many other commitments, performed his duties very much by remote control, relying on Fairbairn and a loyal and dedicated staff on site. Nonetheless, despite the many pressures on his time, Stephenson claimed that he had walked the line fifteen times during its construction.

Moorsom entered the Navy in 1809, rising to the rank of flag-captain to his father who was commander-in-chief at Chatham from 1825 to 1827. Some time after 1827 Moorsom retired from active service on half pay, but remained on the Navy List. He was appointed secretary of the Birmingham Committee of the LBR and together with Richard Creed, the company secretary, supported Stephenson during the crisis over the Kilsby Tunnel. In North Wales he headed the Works Committee based at Chester which supervised the construction and later his maritime experience proved invaluable when the CHR undertook the operation of a fleet of steamers between Holyhead and Kingstown (Dun Laoghaire), which had superseded Howth as a port for Dublin after the opening of the Dublin & Kingstown Railway late in 1834.

The CHR was only one of the hundreds of schemes promoted during the Railway Mania of 1845-1846 but the timing was coincidental, and it promised to be a well-founded project with the enticing prospects of virtually monopolising the traffic between London and Dublin. Headed by the banker, George Carr Glyn, it would not in normal times have expected problems in raising capital. But the years following 1845 were far from normal times and an orgy of speculation depressed the financial markets with 1850 marking the lowest point. Thus throughout its early life the CHR was competing for capital against a swarm of highly speculative ventures which in their failure served to destroy public confidence in railway developments generally.

Despite this expectation, towards the end of 1845 Robert Stephenson's office and even his private house were invaded by would-be railway projectors. Although he could well afford to be selective, Stephenson became engaged in thirty-four schemes, while Brunel contented himself with a modest fourteen. Sir John Macneill led the field with thirty-seven. In total, during the Sessions of 1845 and 1846, the raising of £174 million capital was authorised, or in the region of £10 billion, probably more, at current values.

The Financiers Scent Profits

Prior to 1844, the capitalists of the City of London, the investment bankers of their day, had shown little interest in railway shares and forecast financial disaster for all involved. When they saw the level of dividends paid by successful lines their gloomy views quickly changed and, as a result of them entering the market, the price of shares rose sharply. The public became intoxicated with the idea of the fortunes to be made in railway shares and lost all reason. Samuel Smiles bluntly commented:

> *Folly and knavery were, for a time, completely in the ascendancy. The sharpers of society were let loose and jobbers and schemers became more and more plentiful... Then was the harvest time of scheming lawyers, parliamentary agents, engineers, surveyors and traffic takers, who were ready to take up any railway scheme however desperate and to prove any amount of traffic even when none existed... The result of the labours of Parliament was a tissue of legislative bungling... Committees decided without discrimination: it was a scramble for Bills, in which the most unscrupulous were the most successful.*

The effect on the CHR was unforeseen but, long before the real financial crisis of 1848, the company was facing problems. The original capital authorised in 1844 was £2,100,000 in £50 shares, of which the London & Birmingham was permitted to contribute up to £1,000,000. By May 1845, contracts had been let for nearly £1,000,000, excluding the bridges at Conwy and Britannia, and another £170,000 had been estimated for the acquisition of land. Nearly a year was to pass until in March 1846 the contracts for the masonry of the two bridges were let and it was the following November before the final contracts for the ironwork were placed. Money was flowing out and there would be no return until at least part of the line was opened to traffic. Little wonder that the board was leaning heavily on Stephenson for a start on the tubes.

While contracts had been placed as far back as July 1846 for 8,000 tons of iron, provision had to be made for the necessary workshops and staging where the tubes could be erected. In August the first orders for plates were sent out, and Moorsom together with Fairbairn, Forster and Clark surveyed the erection sites and drawings were put in hand. In January 1847 the sites were pegged out and within a few weeks the staging for two tubes were completed at Menai. At Conwy, Evans had tendered for all works including workshops and staging, the latter being only for a single tube. In March, Benjamin J. Nowell was awarded a contract for cottages at Menai, each to sleep ten men.

With a worsening financial position, for many shareholders resisted or ignored further calls on their shares, strict economy became the order of the day and the board made their feelings known to Stephenson. Difficulties in obtaining supplies of 2ft 4in wide plates for the bottom cells delayed a start at Menai and all supplies were directed to Evans at Conwy, where on 8 April Clark drove the first rivet. It was not until four months later, in August, that Clark performed a similar ceremony at Menai. This delay allowed the company some breathing space to raise further funds and the first delivery of iron to Menai was delayed until the middle of June.

Instructions were given that work on the third and fourth tubes at Menai should be held back and that the construction of the shorter land tubes should not start until 1848. The staging on each shore on which the land spans were to be built was to accommodate only a single tube and then would be moved over for the second. This false economy seems to have been ignored, for in 1848 work was progressing simultaneously on both pairs of tubes. Plans for a 60ft statue of Britannia on the centre tower by John Thomas were wisely shelved. Despite introducing these delays, the directors demanded that the bridge should be opened by August 1849. Secure in his position, Stephenson would make no promises.

The company's bankers were Glyn, Hallifax, Mills & Co., in which the CHR chairman was senior partner. They were also bankers to the LNWR and these and other interlocking interests, including Moorsom's membership of both boards, were beneficial when the CHR found itself in trouble. Nevertheless in October 1848, when the boom had turned to bust and the banks had their own problems, the CHR was faced with a demand for the repayment of a loan for £75,000. Not only was the expenditure on the tubular bridges far in excess of Stephenson's original estimates, but in 1847 a fleet of steamers for the Holyhead to Dublin passage had been ordered at a cost of £200,000 with no prospect of a profit until the line was opened. Even worse, the Admiralty was demanding a contribution of £200,000 towards the new harbour works at Holyhead. In June 1849, a further Act of Parliament allowed additional borrowing, but by August the situation was again desperate and Moorsom threatened to withdraw all services west of Bangor including the steamers.

Whether or not his fellow directors on the LNWR board took Moorsom's threat seriously, they yet again offered a loan of £100,000 and the CHR, for its part, mortgaged the steamers for £25,000. The funds needed to complete the Britannia Bridge were now in place but it would be March 1850 before the first revenue-earning train could cross. When Moorsom announced to a meeting of the CHR board that the line was now open it must have been with a great sense of relief, but the company's troubles were far from over. Nine years later in 1859 the CHR formally amalgamated with the LNWR but lingered on in name only for another twenty years until dissolved by Act of Parliament. In 1851, Samuel Morton Peto became chairman of the CHR, although Moorsom remained a director, and in 1861, for a few months until his death, Moorsom became chairman of the LNWR, rounding off a distinguished career in the service of the company.

Being on the Navy List, although never recalled for active service, Moorsom had enjoyed promotion by stepping into dead men's shoes as was customary. In 1843 he published a treatise on *The principles of naval tactics* and, in 1851, was promoted to rear-admiral, followed by a further rise to vice-admiral in 1857. There is sometimes confusion between Constantine and William Scarfe Moorsom (1804-1863), his younger brother. After leaving the Army, W.S. Moorsom had quite a distinguished career as a railway engineer, leaving to posterity the Lickey Incline as an enduring monument.

Gentleman employees of the Grand Trunk Railway of Canada, 1859. Left: Francis Thompson, architect; seated: believed to be the general manager; standing: unknown, but probably chief clerk; right: Alexander M. Ross, chief engineer.

Six

The Bridge at Conwy:
Alexander McKenzie Ross (1805-1862)

Supervision of the construction of the Chester & Holyhead Railway was shared by two engineers of considerable experience and ability. The section from Conwy to Holyhead was allocated to Frank Forster. The longer section from Chester to Conwy, including the Conwy Bridge, fell to Alexander McKenzie Ross. Ross was born at Scottsburn, Ross-shire, in the Scottish Highlands, but his family moved to Dornoch in Sutherland, where he received a sound education in the Scottish tradition, excelling in the study of mathematics. His first employment was in London with the eminent contractor Hugh McIntosh. For some reason Ross never applied for membership of the Institution of Civil Engineers and consequently was awarded no official obituary, so the details of his career have had to be pieced together from various sources.

His later career as engineer to the Grand Trunk Railway of Canada brought him much public acclaim there but, like the legion of engineers who practised their profession abroad, Ross was later to find himself without honour in his own country. Even more unjustly, he suffered character assassination by George Robert Stephenson and his hangers-on in Westminster after Robert Stephenson's death. Robert himself had greatly respected Ross's abilities from the early days on the North Midland Railway, and would have been horrified at his cousin's display of professional jealousy, though none of the Stephensons were averse to taking undeserved credit on occasion.

One source of biographical detail is an obituary in *The Leader* of Toronto, dated 27 August 1862. Unfortunately, this is a typical eulogy of the period, long on praise and short on facts. It tells little of his early life except that he was born in the Scottish Highlands in 1805. Nonetheless, it is tempting to quote:

> *But Ross was no common man: and in the very wreck of great powers there is a moral grandeur enforcing respect. From the ruin we gather what the shrine once was. By the mental strain which shatters a great mind, we can judge its tendencies and gauge its powers.*

A valuable source is a letter addressed to Hugh Ross, Alexander's brother in London. This letter was from a George Tate, a contractor's engineer, who had worked alongside Ross for much of his working life and was appalled by the treatment Ross had received.

Tate had first met Ross in 1826 when the latter was working for the public works contractor, Hugh McIntosh, who was employed by John Nash, architect to King George IV, and James Morgan, engineer to the Regents Canal Co. They did not meet again until 1832 when Ross was employed by Nash to survey a proposed railway in the Isle of Wight, one of many forgotten early schemes. In 1837 Ross was employed by the Stephensons on the North Midland Railway, where he was placed in charge of the Bull Bridge contract. This was a tricky piece of engineering, where the railway had to burrow under the Cromford Canal and a new aqueduct had to be built without stopping the canal traffic.

The original stone aqueduct, which carried the canal across the valley of the Amber, had been a source of concern from early days and all but two of the arches had been filled with rubble to form an embankment. This treacherous ground prevented any normal tunnelling method being used. Ross devised a cast-iron trough built up from plates which were assembled on a branch of the canal which had been drained to form a dry dock. Once assembled the ends of the trough were sealed off and water admitted to the dock, allowing the trough to float. The finished trough was 150ft long and of sufficient internal size to allow the passage of a canal narrow boat. The trough was floated into position over part of the aqueduct and water admitted allowing it to settle firmly on to the clay puddling of the channel. The joints at the ends were made watertight with clay. This whole operation was carried out in less than twenty-four hours over a Sunday with the agreement of the canal company and water traffic had resumed by Monday. Normal mining techniques were then used to tunnel beneath the trough and a stone arch was built which incorporated the iron trough out of sight within the stonework.``

The Stephensons were much impressed by the success of the work and Robert marked Ross down as an engineer of great potential. Tate then proceeds to tell how, in 1843, Ross worked on the North Wales Mineral Railway under its engineer, Henry Robertson MA. Ross was next involved in the CHR parliamentary survey by Robert Stephenson. When the Bill went before Parliament in 1844, Ross gave evidence on Stephenson's behalf. With the passing of the Act Ross was placed in charge of the design of bridges and other structures on the line. Ross is also credited with designing a bridge across the Foyle at Londonderry and the design of the railway from Bilbao to Madrid. Undoubtedly Ross was an experienced and competent engineer and Stephenson had made an excellent decision in appointing him to the Chester & Holyhead.

His later part in the construction of the Grand Trunk Railway of Canada will be described in the chapter on the Victoria Tubular Bridge at Montréal, where he was joint engineer with Robert Stephenson in name, but solely in charge of all the Canadian operations in practice. The building of several hundred miles of railway through largely virgin territory was entirely Ross's responsibility and in this Stephenson played no part.

Most of the distance along the coast of North Wales was over reasonably level and low-lying country, though liable to occasional flash floods such as the one in August 1879 which washed away the seven-span stone viaduct at Llandulas. The story of how this was replaced within a month by a new steel viaduct, fabricated in the Crewe works using steel from their own furnaces, is a saga in itself though beyond the scope of this history. Ross's job was no sinecure, for the railway in the vicinity of Penmaenmawr involved heavy tunnelling and parts of the line were under constant attack from the sea. His major work, however, was the building of the bridge over the River Conwy.

For several reasons the bridge at Conwy was more important than the far larger and more imposing structure at Menai. The first river crossing at Conwy was Telford's elegant suspension bridge, with a span of 327ft. Being first on the scene had allowed him to make use of a spur of rock just below the castle walls. The railway engineers were less fortunate and the best site available to them, closely paralleling Telford's bridge, still required a span of 400ft and even them some piling was unavoidable under one tower. Floating out the first tube there would allow the tricky operation to be tried in the less turbulent waters of the river, when lessons could be learnt in advance, to stand them in good stead when the time came for the altogether more demanding task at Menai.

It had always been Stephenson's intention that the Conwy tubes should be built first so that they could act as a test bed for the larger Britannia tubes. The directors were not of the same mind. They demanded that both bridges should proceed simultaneously so that there should be no delay in opening the line throughout. At this juncture fate stepped in — no doubt to Stephenson's secret satisfaction. Fairbairn was having much difficulty in obtaining the wider plates needed for the bottom cells of the tubes, particularly those towards mid-span where triple best iron was demanded due to the high stress.

Fairbairn's tests on the model tube had shown that, at least towards the centre of the span, the iron had to be of the highest quality as used for steam boilers. Few ironmasters could meet the specification. The most reliable supplier proved to be G.B. Thorneycroft & Co. of the Shrubbery Ironworks, Wolverhampton. However, a shortage of capital generally following the end of the Railway Mania rather than the failings of the ironmasters may have caused deliveries of iron to be postponed. In the event, initial supplies were concentrated at Conwy, which allowed Evans, the contractor, several months start, and would at least speed up opening of the line as far as Bangor.

William Evans: an Able Contractor

Tenders for fabrication of the ironwork for Conwy were sought some weeks before those for Britannia, probably soon after Mr Blair (Fairbairn's right-hand man at Manchester and always spoken of as Mr Blair — one can imagine him invariably wearing a stovepipe hat around the works) had completed basic working drawings in July 1846. Stephenson was not happy with the tenders received from several well-known firms for building the Conwy tubes, though offers came from as far afield as Scotland. To Stephenson's surprise, William Evans, the contractor for the masonry, expressed a wish to tender, but since he had neither workshops nor machinery, nor even relevant experience, Stephenson was at first reluctant to consider his offer. It was around this time that a young engineer from Lancashire, William Heap, joined the contractor's staff. Heap was keen and willing, and after completion of the Conwy Bridge, he moved with Evans to the Drogheda contract. Later they both turn up in important positions at the Canada Works, and the business Heap founded is still trading under his name today.

It had previously been envisaged that the tubes would be built as sub-assemblies in established shipyards or factories. These sections would be transported by water and finally riveted together on site. Evans saw advantages in carrying out the whole process in one place and offered to provide machinery and workshops at Conwy. The work that Evans had done under his original contract had impressed Stephenson favourably and when Evans submitted a tender of £145,190, including the building of six timber

The rolling mill for wrought iron at the Horsehay Ironworks, Coalbrookdale, around 1850.

pontoons, it was accepted with a mixture of relief and lingering misgivings. Once again events would prove that Stephenson had judged his man wisely.

On 11 June 1846 Fairbairn's drawing office completed the drawings for the workshops, and on 8 July tenders were accepted. In August the sites for the staging and workshops were marked out and work proceeded rapidly. Evans set up a drawing office at Conwy and employed two draughtsmen. He ordered machinery, which at the beginning consisted of a 20hp steam engine, driving three cropping and shearing machines, a vertical drill, a lathe, three fly presses for punching the plates, and two workshop cranes on wheels, together with a number of forges and rivet furnaces. Not least, there were 6in cast-iron stretching beds. When the iron plates were first received from the rolling mill they were not truly flat. In a supreme example of metal bashing, blacksmiths wielding 40lb sledgehammers would coerce the plates into shape, turning them over and repeating the process as often as necessary. At Menai, with five or six times the tonnage of plates to handle, many $\frac{3}{4}$in thick, a set of steam-driven cold rolls was installed.

Labour and Welfare: Physical and Spiritual

There was no tradition of large-scale iron working in the district and the decision to fabricate the tubes entirely on site required skilled labour to be imported. Mare's men came mostly from the Thames shipyards, while Garforth and Evans had Lancashire connections. Either way, there was a very limited prospect of local lodgings, while the fact that Welsh was the first and often the only language of the local people made social interaction with the incomers limited. Unfortunately, they brought with them their restrictive practices and a state of mind previously unknown in a predominantly agricultural area. It fell to Capt. Moorsom to act as mediator when necessary but there is no record of serious labour troubles, apart from one riot, probably because trade generally was at a low ebb and jobs were hard to come by.

To house the incomers a number of cottages, known as 'the huts', were built on the Caernarfon side to accommodate ten men on a double shift basis. The furnishing was far from lavish, consisting of five beds and a table together with basic facilities for cooking. The contract for building the cottages was awarded to J. Nowell, one of the consortium of masons at Menai, in March 1847. Elsewhere on the line the contractor Thomas Jackson provided wooden cottages for his married men and let them at rates which undercut the local landladies, but the innkeepers of Bangor rose up in protest when Jackson also started selling beer. It was hoped that Jackson's cottages would be a good example to the owners of local slate quarries, who only provided primitive stone barracks for their men to occupy during the working week. Crude though they were, the cottages were far better than the turf huts found on other construction sites.

On many lines 'tommy shops' were run by the contractors or their tenants and the employers paid their men with tokens only redeemable at inflated prices in the shops. These were a long-standing abuse not confined to the railway industry. Attempts by Parliament to suppress the practice proved ineffective but on the Chester & Holyhead proper shops, some of which grew quite sizeable, were provided where needed and the men were paid in cash on alternate Saturdays. Only the most essential work was done on Sundays, but the Devil found work for idle hands and forty men working on Anglesey were dismissed for disorderly conduct on the Sabbath.

The local people were mostly deeply religious but the chapels of the various denominations conducted their services mainly in Welsh. To serve those of the Anglican persuasion several churches were quickly built. Further steps were taken to ensure the spiritual welfare of the incomers and eight scripture readers were employed to address the men in their free time and to encourage them to send their children to school. While the company made a contribution towards the wages of the readers, it offered no assistance for the provision of schooling. The Revd T. Jackson was employed to work among the Irish Catholics. These precautions seem to have paid off in the Bangor district at least, for the police reported to the magistrates that eight or ten collegians, students presumably, who had been living in the city for some weeks, had been more riotous and disorderly than six or seven hundred labourers employed within the Bangor Parish in making the Chester & Holyhead Railway.

Records of the quarter sessions show that most offences were very minor, arising from personal disputes, and were dealt with by binding over to keep the peace, though one case involved a fine of £4 or two months' imprisonment for assaulting a police officer. As might be expected there was always petty thieving, for which the Irish were inevitably blamed, and pilfering of tools and material from the contractors was rife. Some defendants were bound in the sum of £50, no small amount in those days, to appear at the next quarter sessions after inquiries had been completed. To discourage the incidence of thieving night watchmen were employed and one of these, John Rowlands, was murdered in 1848. A suspect was arrested but later released for lack of evidence.

It was not all sweetness and light for, although most of the men working on the line were, like the masons, recruited locally, there was a strong Irish contingent at

Penmaenmawr. The Irish were never averse to a good fight among themselves, although it was generally the English navvies who provoked them, and elsewhere, as at Penrith, it could lead to full-scale riots and military assistance being demanded by the civil authorities. The Welsh workers on the Chester & Holyhead were a peaceable crowd, more given to singing than brawling, but at Penmaenmawr in May 1846, they turned against the 300 Irish navvies, whom Jackson had taken on, rose up in a body and drove them off the line. The violence of the conflict was such that the police were helpless and the magistrates read the Riot Act. A troop of soldiers was despatched to the scene but did not arrive for two days by which time tempers had cooled.

Reported deaths on the line were, for the period, surprisingly few, totalling fifteen and they were commemorated on a stone in the churchyard of Llanfairpwllgwyngyll. This stone also records the death from typhus in October 1847 of William Brook of Dewsbury, chief accountant of the contractors for the masonry. Plagues did not spare white-collar workers.

Building of the First Conwy Tube

Construction of the Conwy tubes started when Edwin Clark, professionally assisted by Evans, drove the first rivet on 8 April 1847. According to Samuel Smiles, Evans encountered labour problems at Conwy. The ironworkers had been recruited in England and they brought their radical views with them. Repeal of Pitt's Combination Act of 1825 had permitted the growth of trade unions, and Evans was faced with a 'combination of workmen' which did nothing to aid productivity. Punching the plates was a major bottleneck. The process of marking out and punching was slow and inaccurate and the fly presses, supplied by Richard Roberts of Manchester, could punch only a single $1\frac{1}{8}$in hole in the thicker plates at each operation. Where three or four thicknesses of iron had to be riveted the correct alignment of the holes presented a serious problem and led to extensive use of the reamer.

When Stephenson made one of his occasional visits to the site on 22 July he was generally satisfied with what he found, but he left specific instructions that all holes should be rymered (reamed). As he wrote to Fairbairn: 'This may not be necessary in every case; but as it is difficult to draw a line where the rymer should or should not be used, I though it the safest plan to give an order that all should be done.'

Reaming by hand with no power tools was an arduous task and just how far it was carried out when no one was looking can only be surmised. With slow and inaccurate punching and the additional need for reaming progress was disappointingly slow, and in desperation Evans turned to Roberts and visited him in Manchester to discuss the manufacture of a superior punching machine. Since the pattern of holes varied between batches of plates some quick means of setting up was essential. Roberts had considerable experience of automatic textile machinery, particularly Jacquard looms where the weaving pattern could be controlled by punched cards. In a matter of weeks Roberts had designed and constructed a punching machine operating on the Jacquard principle and offering a far higher accuracy than had been possible hitherto. A description of this highly sophisticated machine occupies many columns of the *Civil Engineers and Architect's Journal*, in August 1848, and it is not too fanciful to regard it as the ancestor of today's numeri-cally controlled machine tools. With the delivery of this machine to Conwy, work proceeded apace. Once set up the machine could punch up to 144 holes in under three minutes, and it became difficult to keep it fully employed. Strangely, Clark makes no mention of a similar machine at Menai.

Richard Roberts (1789-1864) deserves a few words in passing for he was a prolific inventor. The son of a village shoemaker, he moved to the Black Country and thence to Manchester, where in 1816 he set up business as a mechanical engineer. At that date, machine tools were still extremely crude, and his invention of an improved planing machine and a screw-cutting lathe, among many other advances, were accompanied by a greatly improved gas meter. A useful sideline was the supply of cast-iron billiard tables for export to termite-infested countries. It was his invention of an effective self-acting spinning mule that led to an enormous expansion of the Lancashire cotton industry. In 1828 he joined the firm of Sharp Roberts & Co., locomotive builders, who were renowned for the quality of their products. Roberts was awarded a medal at the Great Exhibition of 1851 for his turret clock. Sadly he was a better engineer than businessman, and was taken advantage of by others, and would have died in poverty had it not been for Fairbairn's intervention.

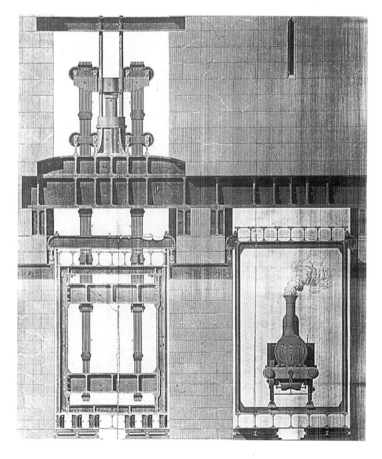

A section of the Conwy tube.

Fabricating
tubes.

The subsequent story of the machine is relevant. After the completion of the second Conwy tube, the machine may have been taken to Menai though Clark does not mention is use there and there may well have been objections from Mare's workers, who had Luddite tendencies. Later Evans removed the machine to Drogheda in Ireland, where he had the contract to build the Boyne viaduct. There it did little work, as the viaduct was a lattice structure with no need for the punching of many large plates. Unfortunately, Evans was virtually bankrupted by problems encountered in the foundations of the central pier. He was offered an opportunity to work for Peto, Brassey & Betts and took the machine with him to the Canada Works at Birkenhead where he was placed in charge of the fabricating shop, with William Heap as second in command. There it was used to punch the plates for the Victoria Tubular Bridge and numerous other bridges of the Grand Trunk Railway of Canada.

The First Tube: Completed and Tested

The first tube was completed on 3 January 1848. It had been decided that, before floating out, it should be subjected to load tests to confirm the accuracy of the design. Since not surprisingly neither Fairbairn nor Clark understood the advanced mathematics for predicting the deflection of a girder under load it was necessary to call once again upon the talents of Eaton Hodgkinson. The means of applying a test load somewhere in the region of 300 tons led to much discussion. The simplest method would have been to seal off the ends of the tube and partly fill it with water, but there was no supply of fresh water in the vicinity, and sea water would have worked its way into every crevice and led to rapid corrosion. There was nothing for it but to use pig iron stacked on the floor of the tube and a total of 236 tons was applied evenly over the centre 300ft of the span according to Clark. Fairbairn, in his book, tabulated a range of loads up to 301 tons. Clark's figure was equal in effect to 278 tons evenly distributed over the full 400ft of the span.

The supports beneath the tube were cut away, leaving it resting on its extreme ends as it would be when in use, and the central deflections were measured as the load was gradually applied. The results were regarded as highly satisfactory in that the full-sized tube behaved as had been predicted from the model tests, and in line with Hodgkinson's calculations. Stephenson had opposed the presence of visitors to view the tests, fearing that some unforeseen and embarrassing problem might arise. On completion of the tests, Faribairn was so elated that, to Stephenson's intense annoyance, he wrote to Moseley, Babbage, Willis, Rennie, and others of similar scientific distinction, reporting the favourable results. Although his presence had been expected, it would seem that problems with a tunnel near Ambergate prevented Stephenson himself from attending the testing and it was rumoured that he also went up to Newcastle on business. In any case, his presence at Conwy would have served little useful purpose though he always like to grace special occasions with his presence.

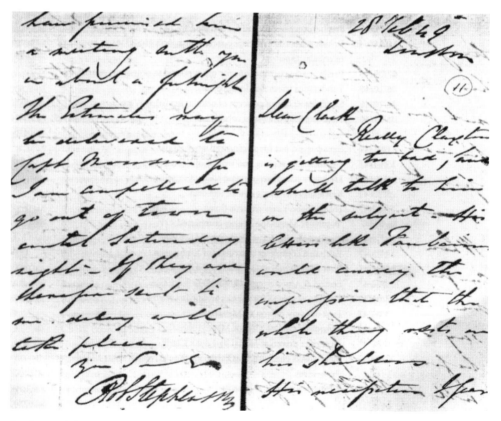

Stephenson's letter.

For his part, Fairbairn was furious when at the beginning of April he received a letter from Stephenson in London saying:

> *It is clear that his [Hodgkinson's] experiments alone have given the true law that governs strength of different sized tubes. Both your plan and my own for calculating the strength are empirical; but Hodgkinson's experiments and the deductions from them, give the true law with remarkable consistency.*

Although apparently satisfactory, the tests were flawed. For a start, Hodgkinson had based his calculated deflection on a value of the modulus of elasticity, a constant arrived at empirically that was somewhat on the low side, thus over-estimating the calculated value for the deflection, and his calculations contained errors due to the limitations of structural theory at the time. In consequence, the deflection under test appeared to be closely in accordance with Hodgkinson's predicted figure, and everyone was satisfied. It came as rather a shock, therefore, when similar tests were carried out on the girder after installation when deflections were found to be some twenty per cent higher than expected. Inevitably, this caused much consternation since it suggested that the Conwy tubes and, more importantly, the Britannia tubes were weaker than had been expected. Measurement of the deflection under load was the criterion used at that time by the railway inspectors to assess the strength of bridges, and so far the empirical design methods had taken no account of the stresses in the iron. Alarm bells began to ring but, by this time, Fairbairn had resigned, as will be explained later. Stephenson and Clark were left on their own to find a solution.

To confuse the issue, in his book Fairbairn reports a quite different set of results, with the quantity and positioning of the test weights varying considerably from Clark's figures.

These tests were expensive to run, with up to 300 tons of pig iron having to be manhandled into place, and it seems most unlikely that two separate series of tests took place when one should have sufficed. This is a mystery which will probably never be resolved.

Assuming that the top did not buckle under compression and Fairbairn's design ensured that the stress in the top was always less than that in the bottom, it was the latter that dictated the strength of the tubes. There was at that time no common ground among engineers as to a maximum safe working stress for wrought iron in tension. After the 1847 Royal Commission on iron had reported early in 1849, a figure of 5 tons per square inch gradually came to be generally accepted, being approximately one quarter of the breaking stress which was taken as 20 tons per square inch with improvements in the quality of iron. This gave a factor of safety of 4, which satisfied all but the most conservative engineers. Tests carried out by Fairbairn ten years later confirmed that fatigue from repeated loadings did not set in until in excess of 7 tons per square inch was repeatedly applied and removed. Beyond that the iron would be permanently damaged and its life shortened. Thus 5 tons per square inch was a conservative working figure and came to be accepted as standard.

The First Conwy Tube Takes to the Water

Stephenson had not been entirely happy with the wooden pontoons built by Evans, and he had required them to be strengthened and the sides raised by 1ft all round. The actual floating out operation was supervised by Capt. Claxton RN, a close friend and colleague of Brunel, while manpower was provided by a crew of sailors from Liverpool.

Capt. Christopher Claxton RN (1790-1868) had been retired from naval service on half-pay and was fortunate in obtaining the position of Quay Warden at the developing port of Bristol in or about 1833. It was in this land-based capacity that he first became acquainted with Isambard Kingdom Brunel, who had considerable interests in the dock system and, although Claxton was sixteen years Brunel's senior, a friendship rapidly developed. Claxton's character was described as being a warm friend but very changeable and very capable of being a devil of an opponent and a hot-tempered Tory. Brunel himself was not the easiest of men to get on with but they appear to have recognised each other's qualities and were to remain lifelong friends and business associates.

Claxton was made managing director of the Great Western Steamship Co. and was aboard the *Great Western* when she sailed for New York on 31 March 1838. A fire on board was fought successfully under Claxton's direction and the ship returned to Bristol for repairs. Eight days later she sailed again to complete her maiden voyage across the Atlantic.

In 1835 Claxton visited Liverpool and Glasgow on a fact-finding tour around the shipyards and prepared a report on iron ships, advocating the advantages of large ships over small. He was then made a member of the building committee for the *Great Britain*. When the ship was completed, she was found to be too wide to pass through the dock gates and Claxton came to the rescue. On her maiden voyage the *Great Britain* was stranded in Dundrum Bay and, with the winter approaching, was given temporary protection during the winter months so that with the advent of better weather she was successfully floated off with no serious damage. Brunel's offer of Claxton's services was welcomed by Stephenson who had no one of comparable maritime experience.

The floating out of the finished tube was generally uneventful under Claxton's able direction. After the improvements required by Stephenson, the six pontoons, three at each end of the tube, had a total lifting capacity of 2,760 tons, while the estimated weight of the tube was only 1,147 tons. There had been some delay in cutting away the staging and, though Stephenson had been on site superintending operations since 20 February, it was 6 March, a Monday and blessed with glorious weather, when floating out commenced. To the cheers of a large crowd, the tube was landed almost under the lifting tackle and the pontoons were flooded and towed away. A band marched over the top of the tube. It took until 11 March to position the tube into its precise location for lifting and not before then could Stephenson finally relax. The perils of lifting were still to come. Clark, who had lost part of a big toe in an accident, could only watch proceedings from a carriage on Telford's bridge.

There were no serious hitches during lifting and the hydraulic presses performed admirably. The lift had taken three days but the tube was not finally bedded in until 16 April. Two days later Stephenson drove the first train to cross. Towards the end of the month Capt. Simmons RE of the railway commissioners made his inspection and in due

Preparation for the
second lift at Conwy.

course reported very favourably. After crossing swords with Stephenson the previous
year over the inadequacies of the Dee Bridge, he was no doubt doubly cautious. The
second tube was not floated until 12 October, when the whole performance was accomplished in less than an hour and almost without incident, watched as before by a large
crowd. The lifting was marred by a crack developing in one of the cast-iron crossheads
to which the lifting chains were attached. Providentially, the crack became no worse
while the lift was cautiously completed, but a major disaster could easily have occurred.
Lessons were learnt from this incident and extra precautions taken at Britannia where
wrought iron crossheads were substituted.

The line was now complete as far as Bangor and revenue-earning traffic could start,
relieving to some extent the pressures on the company's over-stretched finances.
Completion of the first tube at Britannia was still over a year in the future and the resident
director, Capt. Moorsom RN, would be hard pressed to ensure that the necessary funding
was in place to complete the line to Holyhead.

Floating out the second tube at Conwy, 12 October 1848.

As soon as the first Conwy tube had been floated out, Evans set about restoring the working platform for fabrication to proceed on the second tube. This time things moved much faster, for the automatic punching machine was available from the start. Work on the second tube was completed and floating out took place without a great deal of fuss on 12 October 1848 and, by 16 December, it was ready for traffic. Capt. Simmons made his inspection on 2 January 1849. The line from Chester to Bangor was now complete but it would be nearly another fifteen months before the first train ran through to Holyhead. Meanwhile, mail and passengers were taken by road over Telford's bridge where they joined a local train waiting at Llanfair.

Blessed with an innovative and competent main contractor like William Evans at the Conwy Bridge, Alexander Ross encountered no serious problems. Elsewhere on the line around Penmaenmawr, but also at several other places along the North Wales coast, it was a very different story. Storm damage to the sea walls necessitated rebuilding part as a viaduct, allowing the force of the waves to expend itself on the beach behind. To quote from Samuel Smiles:

> Mr Stephenson confessed that if a long tunnel had been made in the first instance through the solid rock of Penmaen Mawr, a saving of from £25,000 to £30,000 would have been effected. He was ready enough to admit the errors he had committed in the original design of this work; but he said he had always gained more information from studying the causes of failures and endeavouring to surmount them, than he had done from easily-won successes. Whilst many of the latter had been forgotten, the former were indelibly fixed in his memory.

There can be no doubt that the fall of the Dee Bridge had proved a chastening experience for Stephenson. But was it not his father George who had amended the line, as recommended by Francis Giles, in order to reduce the amount of tunnelling?

With the completion of the line between Conwy and Chester Alexander Ross had finished what he had set out to do and he handed over the maintenance to Hedworth Lee, who was made the resident engineer. It was in 1852 that Ross was invited by Brassey, Peto, Betts and Jackson, promoters of the Grand Trunk Railway of Canada, to visit that country and carry out a survey. That story will be told in the chapter on the Victorian Bridge, the last and largest of the few.

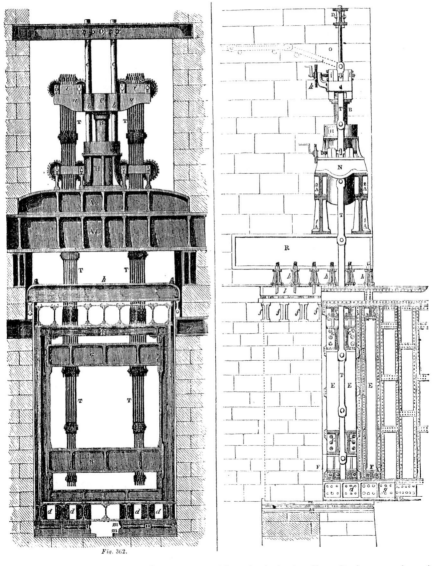

Fig. 362.

Fairbairn's lifting apparatus as used at Conwy with a single hydraulic cylinder at each end.

Fifty Years On

The last decade of the nineteenth century was to prove a period of great change in bridge and locomotive design. The dynamic forces exerted on bridges by the passage of a train had been dismissed by an influential body of British engineers as nothing more than figments of an over-active imagination. In America and in India, and doubtless on the Continent too, there was a somewhat inglorious history of bridge failures in the 1880s – many of which attributed to the overloading and overstress from ever-heavier locomotives. While the Midland Railway was endowed with a heritage of small locomotives, the LNWR had less enthusiasm for double heading and sought more powerful motive power for its flagship services like the Irish Mail.

Thanks to Edwin Clark, or whoever had introduced him to the magic properties of the continuous beam, it had ensured that the Britannia tubes were assured an ample reserve of strength. Not so at Conwy with its single span: by 1899 it was clear that something had to be done and this was achieved by inserting cast-iron columns in the bed of the river, 50ft out from each abutment. This reduction in span has ensured that the Conwy Bridge, the last of few such bridges, should survive well into the twenty-first century, and the introduction of diesel locomotives has done much to reduce dynamic loading.

The following notes are a gross simplification of a highly complex subject. It had been the practice for many years to apply balance weights to the driving wheels of locomotives in order to balance out the horizontal forces set up by the reciprocating movements of the pistons and motion. While near perfect balancing could be achieved, it was not at first appreciated that the rotation of the balance weights also set up unbalanced vertical forces which tended on each revolution to lift the driving axle against the springs or to bring it thumping down on the track – the dreaded hammer-blow (a term coined in India in the early twentieth century). A judicious proportioning of the balance weight would give a reasonable compromise between the two effects, but in a two-cylinder locomotive perfect balancing was unobtainable and some degree of hammer-blow had to be endured.

The effect on track and bridges was that the apparent weight of a locomotive was more – sometimes far more than its dead weight. Around the turn of the twentieth century engineers had to face up to this problem, and there was an orgy of new bridges or bridge strengthening at great expense. The locomotive engineers had to modify some of their new designs to meet the demands of the civil engineers, often leading to strained relations in the hierarchy. Even more embarrassing was the discovery that a few locomotive classes were beyond redemption and had to be scrapped discreetly before their due time. This must have called for some creative accounting!

The matter was finally laid to rest in the late 1920s by the Bridge Stress Committee, chaired by Prof. C.E. Inglis. In 1935 he published the definitive treatise on the subject. Among the many experiments commissioned was one on the wheels of a locomotive in motion. It was observed with astonishment and deep concern that under certain conditions the wheels would rise off the rails almost to the height of the flanges. Those who had discounted the dynamic effects of hammer-blow were duly convinced.

Seven

The Benefits of Continuity

The subject of continuous beams has been referred to previously; it is not something that is widely understood even among professional engineers. It is rarely encountered now since, though a valuable principle if correctly applied, it fell into disrepute because of its misapplication, particularly in America where it led to a string of bridge failures in the late nineteenth century.

Although the practical application of continuous beams goes back a long way, at least to the time of Galileo and probably earlier, Navier in France was the first to make a scientific study of the principle. In England, Thomas Tredgold (1788-1829) approached strength of materials from a mainly practical point of view and, writing in 1820 in a discourse on floors, he advocated using bridging joists in long lengths so that they extend over several binding joists and have increased strength and stiffness. He bases this on the work of Belidor (1697-1761), who wrote a mathematical textbook for military engineers published as early as 1729. Just what was this magical principle which played so great a part in the long-term success of the Britannia Bridge?

At its simplest, a beam in one length resting across three or more supports is stronger than shorter beams laid end to end over the same supports. This assumes that all the points of support remain in line and early bridge failures often arose from settlement in the piers, which was particularly dangerous with short spans. As an example, a continuous beam will take up the shape shown in the diagram representing the Britannia Bridge (p.84), whereas the four individual tube sections would lie as shown under their own weight.

The mathematics of the continuous beam were first investigated by Navier in 1826, and they were brought to England by Henry Moseley (1801-1872), who had studied at Abbeville in France. Moseley was a man of many parts and held a Cambridge MA in mathematics. In 1831 he became Professor of Natural Philosophy and Astronomy at Kings College, London and a Fellow of the Royal Society in 1839. In 1844 Moseley was appointed one of Her Majesty's first Inspectors of Schools and in 1853 he was made a Canon of Bristol Cathedral. In 1843 he published an original book, the first in its field, *Mechanical principles of engineering and architecture*, which included among some new and very valuable material, an examination of continuous beams based on Navier's earlier work. The book was probably more widely owned than understood, for its use of the calculus made it incomprehensible to the practising engineers of the day. At that time British engineers were derided by their continental cousins for their lack of theoretical knowledge, but on the other hand greatly envied for their ready access to vast sums of capital.

At Britannia it was intended from the start to join the tubes end to end with junction pieces within each tower after erection, but this would merely have held them together and would have done nothing to assist in reducing the effect of each one's self-weight. It is true that under this condition any applied load would have been shared to some extent, but this would have done nothing to relieve the greater part of the stresses at mid-span arising from the great weight of the tubes themselves. Clark's aim was to reduce these mid-span stresses and thereby increase the stiffness and the load bearing properties of the tubes.

There is no clear evidence as to why or when or by whom the idea of structural continuity was introduced at Menai. Fairbairn had designed his tubes to be self-supporting independently and had found neither the time nor any necessity to carry out tests on continuous beams. Stephenson had spoken of tests to bring the upper part of the tubes into tension but offered no suggestions as to how this might be achieved. Fairbairn was under too much pressure to devote precious time to what he regarded as a flawed concept, and he was quite satisfied in his own mind that simple beams would be adequate. When presented later with the idea of continuity he was willing to accept that there might be something in it but he was very sceptical of William Pole's mathematical demonstration, first made public in March 1850 during a heated debate on John Fowler's bridge at Torksey over the Trent. All that can be said with some degree of certainty is that continuity was introduced after Fairbairn's resignation and before work started on the short land spans in November 1848. It is conceivable that Brunel could have mentioned the idea to Stephenson but it was 1849, long after the decision at Menai, when Brunel carried out his own experiments on continuous beams in connection with the planned bridge at Chepstow.

The Conwy Tube Put to the Test

What may have caused serious concern were the tests carried out on the first Conwy tube before erection. Hodgkinson had been called in soon after the first Conwy tube was started to calculate the expected deflection under load, which was far beyond Clark's ability and even Hodgkinson found himself at the cutting edge of structural theory. Great credit is due to him for what he achieved although there were errors in his calculations. The introduction of stresses had not been necessary in Fairbairn's work, nor in Hodgkinson's own early work, and it was not until the late 1840s that the calculation of stresses became more generally used in girder design.

According to Clark's figures, not published until late in 1850, the Conwy tube, unloaded, was stressed to 4.62 tons per square inch in the bottom but with an applied static working load of 1 ton per foot run, this stress increased to 5.6 tons per square inch. This was somewhat high by later standards, though there was no general consensus among engineers in 1850 and this gave a safety factor (on Airy's principle) of 3.3. But the Conwy Bridge could be strengthened with intermediate piers, as happened later under the auspices of the LNWR in 1899 when train loads had greatly increased, but during the first fifty years high stress gave no cause for immediate concern. The Britannia Bridge presented an altogether more serious problem with its greater span.

At Britannia the weight of the tube alone produced a maximum stress in the bottom of 5.62 tons per square inch, and the addition of a live load of 1 ton per foot run increased this to 7.24 tons per square inch, giving a factor of safety of 2.47. Furthermore, the experiments carried out for the 1847 Royal Commission had recommended a maximum stress of about 6.2 tons per square inch if fatigue problems were to be avoided. Even taking into account the fact that the load at that date would never exceed $\frac{1}{2}$ ton per foot run in practice, the stress would still be 6.42 tons per square inch, the factor of safety now being only 2.9. What of the future? Thus the minds of Stephenson and Clark must have been concentrated on the benefits of continuity since there was no solution short of redesigning the tubes, with the first already more than half completed. With no evidence from any source all this must of necessity be speculative. Although William Pole, who was to further develop Moseley's work, had returned from India only at the end of 1847, he had yet to become recognised as a mathematician of great ability. Since Moseley was a personal friend and adviser to Fairbairn, Stephenson would have been reluctant to call on his services which would have led to some loss of face.

Clark, probably with the help of his colleague C.H. Wild, who had a better grasp of structural matters than most of his contemporaries, may have put forward the idea of converting the tubes into a structurally continuous beam. The beauty of this scheme was that the bending moments at mid-span would be reduced by creating reverse bending moments over the piers. In theory, under ideal conditions, the load carrying capacity of a beam could be doubled by this action. But, like a free lunch, there was a hidden price to pay and many pitfalls to be encountered in putting theory into practice.

The tubes had been designed to rest on their supports in the towers with the gap between the ends being filled later with junction pieces. To counteract the deflection at mid-span a camber of nine inches had been provided while building, in the expectation that once erected the soffits of the tubes would be straight and level. Owing to the great weight of a tube, part of the erection platform at Conwy gave way, and the 8in camber allowed there could only be restored by dint of heroic efforts with sledgehammers and wedges.

Clark's real problem lay in the design of the ends of the tubes, where no allowance had been made for bending, and the introduction of reverse bending over the towers led to compression in the bottom cells and tension in the top for which Fairbairn's design made no provision. The greatest danger lay in crushing the bottom cells over the bearings, but this was countered by providing cast-iron pillars within the cells and frames within the tubes. The top cells already incorporated an extra cross-section of iron to offset buckling from the effects of compression and could be expected to stand limited tension without ill effect. At the Britannia tower full continuity could not be attained without certain damage to the tubes and Clark had to content himself with balancing the mid-span bending moment with the reverse bending moment in the tower, or at least as near as he could estimate. Clark settled on a lift of $14\frac{5}{8}$in on the short spans and this was achieved by building the short tubes on a platform raised at the abutment end to avoid jacking up later. At the Britannia tower, when the two main tubes were in position, he measured the angle between the ends of the tubes and estimated how much one tube would need to be lifted to halve this angle. He reckoned that a lift of $31\frac{1}{2}$in at the Caernarfon tower would suffice instead of the 54in required in theory to give perfect continuity.

Ideally the first connection should have been made at the Britannia Tower C but, to avoid delay while the Caernarfon tube was being positioned, he made his first connection at the Anglesey Tower B. The junction piece was inserted between the two tubes and the short tube rolled into place and joined up. With the Caernarfon tube in place

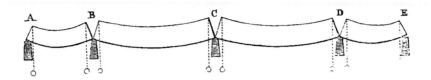

A diagram of the Britannia tubes before they were jointed.

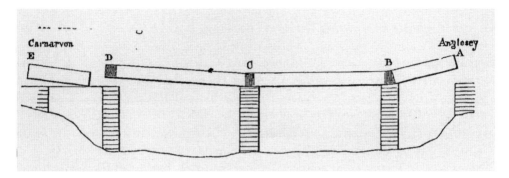

A diagram showing how the Britannia tubes were raised before they were joined into a continuous beam.

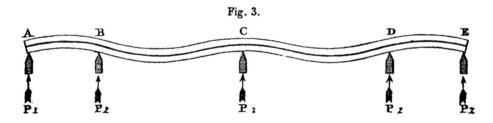

A diagram showing the shape adopted by the Britannia tubes after being made continuous.

and the lifting gear still in position in the land tower, this tube was lifted to the required height at D and the connection made within the Britannia Tower. Unfortunately, this procedure called for a reassessment of the required lift at the Caernarfon abutment, but Clark was prepared to take a chance. As he wrote:

> The calculation of this would be very complicated but we are justified in assuming that the tube was made perfectly continuous at this point… Therefore it appears that the tube may be considered as made continuous at B and D (the two land towers) but falling short of continuity at C (the Britannia tower) by a certain known amount.

This was taking a slightly optimistic view, but Prof. T.M. Charlton has commented:

That statement is not strictly correct both with the restoration of the conditions which full continuity would have afforded at B and D and with reference to the conditions at C being modified by 'a certain known amount'. The latter seems to have been a judicious estimate... Having regard, however, to the errors of magnitude involved and the strains measured, it seems probable that the engineers were justified in their conclusions... Certainly, they seem to have adopted a sound procedure on a scientific basis to which the long life of the bridge in increasingly severe conditions is adequate testimony.

How far Clark had actually achieved his aims was uncertain. The figures quoted to Capt. Simmons when the first tube was being inspected imply that the mid-span bending was reduced to about 0.58 of what it would otherwise have been. The bridge stood, carrying an increasing weight of traffic, until in the 1960s a demand for the use of tank wagons of 102 tonnes gross weight led to a detailed investigation by the British Railways Research Department. By the extensive use of hydraulic load cells and mechanical strain gauges it was established that the reverse bending over the towers was close to what Clark had hoped for, but that this did differ slightly at the two land towers which also was expected. The conclusion reached was that the 102-tonne tank wagons could be used without restriction, a tribute to all who had designed and built the bridge nearly 120 years before. Sadly, before the bridge could be put to the test, Fate intervened and a devastating fire destroyed it in 1970.

The introduction of continuity at Britannia at such an advanced stage received little publicity. Fairbairn's book published early in 1849 naturally made no mention of it. Latimer Clark's pamphlet of 1849, hurriedly produced as an exercise in public relations to offset Fairbairn's book, was silent on the subject. When Capt. Simmons was inspecting the bridge on 15 March 1850, his attention was drawn to the alleged benefits of continuity by Stephenson and the Inspector's report states:

...advantage has been taken, by the continuity of the beams to bring the top into a state of tension to a considerable extent, reducing in a great degree the central strains which would otherwise be brought on the metal. It is difficult to define the exact amount of this benefit, but it is undoubtedly considerable and has been estimated by Mr Stephenson as reducing the greatest strain upon the metal from 5 tons 3 cwt to 3 tons per square inch, or increasing the strength in a like ratio.

Since Simmons had no means of checking these figures and was satisfied with the deflection of the tubes under load he held his peace. With memories of the Dee Bridge affair the two men must have been wary of each other and Simmons already had a fight on his hands with John Fowler and virtually the whole civil engineering establishment by condemning as inadequate Fowler's bridge over the Trent at Torksey. Coincidentally the subject of continuity was creating a furore at meeting of the Civils as, at the end of the previous year, Simmons had refused to allow this Lincolnshire bridge to be opened. His grounds for the rejection were insufficient strength and poor workmanship. In the course of his argument, he claimed that the maximum stress upon wrought iron should not exceed 5 tons per square inch. While in years to come that would indeed be the figure adopted by the Board of Trade, it had no authoritative backing in 1850 and Simmons found himself out on a limb.

Field-Marshal to be, John Lintorn Arabin Simmons (1821-1903), was not a man to be deterred by shot and shell from a bunch of noisy civilians, however eminent, and he stood his ground until his superiors at the Board of Trade, coming under strong commercial pressures from the Great Northern and other railway interests, pulled the rug from under him. There is reason to suspect that he did not take kindly to life as a civil servant, and in 1854, when he went on leave, he joined the Turkish Army on the Danube, refusing to return to England when ordered. Later he went on to serve with the Turks in the Crimea. His act of insubordination seems to have done his career no harm, for he went on to give distinguished service in the Royal Engineers for another twenty-four years and finally served as Governor of Malta from 1884 to 1888.

John Fowler, the designer and engineer responsible, produced many high powered witnesses to support his view that continuity over the central pier provided the extra strength required. It was not so much that the members of the Civils were worried about young Fowler, but from Brunel down they rose as a body to oppose the Government interference in technical matters, which as they claimed, had done so much harm on the continent. To them, Simmons was a busybody who needed to be put in his place. To support Fowler's case practical experiments were carried out by Wild, and recourse was had to the mathematical abilities of William Pole. Stephenson wisely kept his head down and did not attend the meetings; George Parker Bidder held the fort on his behalf. Brunel, the arch critic of government interference, wrote privately to Simmons, sympathising with his technical arguments.

William Pole: a Victorian Polymath

William Pole (1814-1900) was a typical Victorian polymath, an unusually competent practical mathematician, a musician and organist of considerable talent, a keen astronomer and for light relief he became a world authority on the game of whist. In addition, he was fluent in several languages and was made a Fellow of the Royal Society for his work on colour blindness. Add to that quite a formidable personality with no respect for fools. Born in Birmingham, Pole became an assistant to Henry Moseley when the latter was investigating the Cornish pumping engine. After completing Moseley's work for him and writing a massive treatise on the subject, Pole was offered the post of Professor of Engineering at Elphinstone College, Bombay, which trained young Indians, mostly Parsees, for the lower-ranking engineering duties in the public works department. After four years, poor health brought on by the Bombay climate forced Pole to return to England where he took up various employments before establishing himself as a consulting engineer.

His importance in this context was that he produced an elegant mathematical exposition of the theory of continuity as originally developed by his mentor, Moseley, and later, at Stephenson's request, expanded this to cover conditions at Britannia. In fact, he wrote

William Pole MusDoc, FRS, MICE
(1814-1900).

all those parts of Clark's book involving serious mathematics and structures. Unfortunately, theory and practice do not always coincide since, as Fairbairn commented, mathematicians live in a perfect world. However, Pole proved to the satisfaction of all but the sceptics like Fairbairn that continuity at Torksey (in fact an unplanned spin–off from the mode of erection) had reduced the stresses in the bridge in a ratio of 3:2, reducing the stresses as a result to just within Simmons' parameter.

It should be explained that the Torksey Bridge had two equal spans of 130ft, and it was assembled in one place on the western approach and rolled out over the river. There was nothing in the design to suggest that it had been intended as a continuous beam. Although built by Fairbairn, Fowler had introduced modifications to which Fairbairn objected. Pole's figures must be taken as a theoretical exercise.

Where conditions are suitable the benefits of continuous spans are widely recognised, but Molesworth's famous handbook sounds a note of warning:

The proper use of continuous bridges of any magnitude demands sound and expert knowledge which sometimes lacking in the past has brought such structures into disrepute. But there is no doubt that for spans above 200 feet, especially with heavy loading and provided that suitable foundations can be obtained they merit serious consideration on account of their inherent advantages over simple spans.

Eight

A Sad Mishap at the Dee Bridge

The early months of 1847 marked considerable progress both at Conwy and Menai. Work on the bottom of the first Conwy tube was well advanced by late May and the stagings and workshops at Menai were complete and awaiting their first delivery of iron. The financial climate, however, was unpromising, for the aftermath of the Railway Mania was to depress the money markets for several years and public confidence in even the soundest railway ventures was at a low ebb. Although contracts for most of the iron had been let the previous year, delays in the supplies to Menai allowed some breathing space, and priority was given to completing the Conwy Bridge and line through to Bangor when additional revenue-earning traffic would commence.

Stephenson, for his part, was relieved by the prospect of carrying out trials on the first Conwy tube before work became too far advanced at Menai. In the event, this proved fortunate. However, any satisfaction that Stephenson may have felt was shattered when, on 24 May 1847, one girder of his trussed cast-iron girder bridge over the Dee at Chester collapsed beneath a train, resulting in five deaths. While it is most unlikely that Stephenson himself took any part in the detailed design of the bridge, he had nonetheless approved the choice of structure, and as engineer-in-chief stood accountable in law. There was every prospect of his indictment on a charge of manslaughter, not murder as some would have had it, and his reputation and career were in jeopardy as never before.

The Dee Bridge lies about a mile west of Chester Station, and carries the line at an angle of fifty-one degrees across the river to Saltney Junction, about half a mile beyond the river on a rising gradient. The bridge was built by the CHR but was initially used only by contractors' traffic and trains of the Shrewsbury & Chester Railway, formerly the North Wales Mineral Railway, which opened on 4 November 1846 as far as Ruabon. It would be another year before the bridge was used by the first CHR trains running as far as Rhyl. The line left Chester by a single-span trussed cast-iron bridge over the Ellesmere Canal, and was carried on a viaduct of forty-three brick arches across the low-lying ground known as the Roodee, home to Chester racecourse. There it swung westwards on a curve of two miles' radius over the Dee.

Stephenson's first proposal was for a brick bridge of five arches of 60ft each, but the soft river bed offered a poor foundation and a lighter structure was considered advisable. Stephenson opted for the trussed cast-iron girders of which he and his friend, George Parker Bidder, had previous satisfactory experience. Never before though had anyone attempted a clear span of 98ft with this type of girder and the modifications incorporated to attain this span were to lead to its downfall. Just who instigated them will probably never be known.

On 4 February 1846 Fairbairn had written to Stephenson advocating a tubular (box) girder structure at Chester and had prepared drawings which were shown to him. For one

The fallen Dee Bridge at Chester on 24 May 1847 – note the tender off the rails on the left and damage to the bridge abutments.

reason or another, but probably because they were still at a very early stage of development, these plans were rejected, with unforeseen and unfortunate consequences. The gossip of the day attributed the design of the Dee Bridge to Bidder, and he would doubtless have recommended it in the light of previous success with this type of structure. However, he was at the time fully engaged on the North Staffordshire Railway where such bridges were not used and he took no other part in the CHR where Stephenson alone was in charge. Nor was the detailing of the bridge at Chester comparable with any others Bidder had built previously.

On the face of it, the principle was simple: a single cast girder to span 98ft would, for a start, have needed to be at least 8ft deep at mid-span to give a span:depth ratio of $12\frac{1}{2}$:1, about as slim as it was wise to go. The weight of such a casting would have been enormous and it would have been virtually impossible to cast without flaws or cooling cracks. Then there was the matter of transport and handling with the techniques available in 1846. Designers of cast-iron building frames had already faced this problem, albeit for much smaller spans, and had introduced wrought iron trussing bars, and as early as 1832 C.B. Vignoles had applied this principle successfully to two bridges of 45ft span over the Leeds & Liverpool Canal. Several years later Stephenson and Bidder had seized on the idea to solve their problems on the Northern & Eastern Railway, and later the London & Blackwall, again apparently with complete success. In all they had built or were building a score of these bridges prior to 1847 and a similar number were built or planned by other engineers like John Hawkshaw and John Fowler.

Reconstruction at Menai.

Each span for each track consisted of two girders cast in three nearly equal lengths, which were bolted end-to-end. Multiple wrought-iron flat bars were attached to raised extensions at each end and passed downwards past the top flange and web almost to the level of the bottom flange at points one third way from each end. There they were linked to similar horizontal bars by pin connections. The thinking behind this seems to have been that the load imposed by the girder at the pin connections would be transferred back by the sloping tendons to the points of attachment over the piers. What actually took place was very different because the end connections at Chester, unlike all the similar bridges elsewhere, were raised well above the top flange. Bending forces set up reduced what should have been a factor of safety of six to less than two even without a load on the girders.

The interactions between the wrought-iron tendons and the cast girder were far more complex than had been imagined and at Chester the designer had, in all innocence, made two fatal errors. Firstly, he had attached the ends of the sloping tendons at too high a level above the neutral axis and, secondly, he had used jacking screws instead of firm pin joints at the junctions of the tendons. Thus, the horizontal tendons did nothing to share the tension in the bottom flange of the casting. Even more seriously, the pull in the sloping tendons drew the points of attachment together – like a suspension bridge without backstays – and added to any bending moment in the cast girder rather than relieving it.

The main castings and probably the wrought ironwork too, were supplied by the Horseley Ironworks of Tipton, but it is unlikely that they possessed the expertise to undertake the detailed design of parts other than the castings which were their speciality. These were proportioned in line with the experimental work of Eaton Hodgkinson and, if correctly applied, should have offered an adequate load-carrying capacity.

If the finger has to be pointed at any individual it has to be Thomas Longridge Gooch, a faithful and much put-upon servant of the Stephensons and engineer of the recently built Trent Valley Railway, where six trussed girder bridges were built, although none exceeded 70ft span. It is perhaps significant that Gooch was later employed to devise a means of strengthening the Dee Bridge and other bridges of the type. Although Capt. Coddington RE had passed the Trent Valley bridges for service, the failure of the Dee Bridge caused the opening of the line to be postponed until strengthening had taken place. The Dee Bridge itself was approved by Maj.-Gen. Pasley RE, the Inspector General of Railways, and there is every reason to believe that as usual he carried out his duties to the best of his considerable abilities.

The Fatal Day

On the morning of 24 May 1847, Stephenson inspected the bridge and found nothing amiss, but he was concerned that the wooden deck might be set on fire by hot cinders and he instructed Betts, the contractor, to lay about 5in of ballast which was quickly done. No consideration was given to the additional load on the girders and it is beyond doubt that it was this additional load that precipitated the failure. While Stephenson was under the false impression that there was an adequate factor of safety, it was still an act of folly to impose this extra loading without considering the consequences.

That evening, the 6.15 p.m. train for Ruabon left Chester five minutes late. It had been a fine summer's day and many people were either walking in the Roodee or fishing on the river and were later available to give eyewitness evidence at the inquest. The driver, James Clayton, almost certainly would have put on speed as he approached the bridge to take a run at the bank on the Saltney side and would have already opened the regulator. As his locomotive reached the centre of the western span he later gave evidence that he felt it rear up and he threw the regulator wide open. The locomotive had enough momentum to reach the abutment but the tender derailed and broke its coupling, throwing the fireman on to the rails where he died instantly. The carriages broke free from the tender, which remained on the abutment, and ran back, falling 36ft into the river. Three passengers were killed in the fall, one died later in hospital and eight were injured. Sure that his fireman was dead, Clayton drove his tenderless locomotive to Saltney and gave the alarm and at once returned to Chester over the undamaged side of the Bridge. Fortunately, the tide was low, otherwise more might have died and the injured were speedily dragged from the water by bystanders and conveyed to the Infirmary where medical staff had been alerted.

The Chester & Holyhead Co. had done little to ingratiate itself with the citizens of Chester. Armed with the powers granted to it by Act of Parliament, it had paid scant attention to local sensibilities and met any serious complaints with threats of litigation. Even its local agent, Mr Munt, was described at the inquest as being a very rude young man. Feelings in the city ran high. In addition, Henry Robertson MA, engineer of the Shrewsbury & Chester, whose train had been lost, had no doubt in his own mind and rightly so as it transpired, that the bridge was fundamentally unsound in design. Prior to the inquest, he made these views widely known in Chester and the public feeling against the CHR was further aroused.

The Chester Inquest

The proceedings in the Coroner's Court were reported almost verbatim by the *Chester Chronicle* and its editor added his own tart comments in leading articles. A more colourful account was given later by F.R. Conder, who had been a pupil under Charles Fox on the London & Birmingham Railway, but after a not altogether successful career in railway contracting he had turned to high-class journalism. To quote Conder:

> *The subject excited great interest at the time and the scene in which the practised skill of the advocate, and the whole tact and authority of Stephenson and Locke united were bent to disprove actual fact, was one which hardly needed the additional novelty of the appearance in court of one of the bravest and coolest men in the world, trembling like an aspen, to fix it indelibly on the recollection.*

The Coroner's Court was convened in Chester Town Hall. A jury was sworn in and advised that their duty was to establish the cause of death and not to point a finger of blame. Stephenson was only a witness and not in the dock, although the foreman of the jury, Sir Edward Walker, was clearly aiming to put him there in due course. The remaining jurors were all respectable tradesmen of the city and doubtless hand picked. The Mayor and several of the magistrates were also in attendance as well as a host of interested observers.

Stephenson had strong professional support. As Conder reported, to give him his due his natural instinct was to accept responsibility but Stephenson was strongly dissuaded from this suicidal course by Mr Tyrrell, solicitor of the company, who was prepared to admit nothing. Joseph Locke put aside his long-standing quarrel with George Stephenson and supported his old friend Robert. Thomas Gooch and Charles Blacker Vignoles also gave evidence in Robert's favour. This 'cloud of engineers', declared the editor of the *Chronicle*, was there to obscure the issue rather than to clarify it.

Stephenson's argument, when presenting his evidence, was that the tender had left the rails and slewed across the track, striking the girder sideways and breaking it. Locke offered the same opinion after examining the wreckage, although the evidence in fact was slight. He did, however, express misgivings about the design of the bridge which, he declared, he would not have adopted himself. Vignoles and Gooch both supported the view that a lateral blow had broken the girder but did not commit themselves further. Maj.-Gen. Pasley was so overcome that his evidence was almost inaudible but he was reported to say that he had examined the bridge carefully and could see no fault, and that he was aware of many similar bridges giving satisfactory service. He could see no reason

Gen. Sir Charles William Pasley RE, FRS (1780-1861). After a distinguished career in the Royal Engineers, he was appointed Chief Inspecting Officer of Railways, 1842-1846. He was promoted to the rank of General in 1860.

to condemn it, although with what he now knew he would not pass it again – an honest admission. It was indeed a tragedy that Pasley, who had devoted much of a distinguished career in the Royal Engineers to scientific studies, being elected a Fellow of the Royal Society in 1816 and who was an officer of conspicuous bravery, should have become embroiled in this affair right at the end of an honourable career.

Pasley had enjoyed a long career in military engineering and fought as ADC to Sir John Moore at Corunna. He was badly wounded at the siege of Flushing and after a year's convalescence he started the School of Military Engineering in 1812 with encouragement from Wellington and was its director until 1841. He was remarkable, perhaps for any period, in insisting that the men who served under him were given due credit for their contribution. In 1842 Pasley was appointed as Chief Inspecting Officer of Railways and held his post until he retired in 1846 when reorganisation took place.

The most significant evidence came from Thomas Jones, publican and milkman. He said that he was crossing the Grosvenor Road bridge, upstream from the railway bridge, and had rested his cans to watch the train crossing the bridge. He stated:

> When the train got on the furthest arch on the Saltney side, I observed a crack open in the middle of the girder; the engine and tender were about the centre; the crack opened from the bottom; the engine had passed the crack and the tender was right upon it; the engine and tender went on and I saw the tender give a rise-up; the carriages gave a jump and fell backward…

This, together with a most detailed examination and tests reported by Capt. Simmons RE, and the eminent civil engineer James Walker, acting on the instruction of the Board of Trade, was more than enough to destroy the theories of the 'cloud of engineers'. It also tends to support the views that, contrary to received wisdom, the centre break was caused by excessive tension in the bottom flange. The break in the girder did not show the classic sign of a compression failure, where an V-shaped piece would have been thrown out of the top.

The jury gave their verdict, the most important finding being:

> *We are further unanimously of the opinion, that the aforesaid girder did not break from any lateral blow of the engine, tender, carriage or van, or from any fault in the masonry or abutments; but from its being made of a strength insufficient to bear the pressure of quick trains passing over it.*

To Stephenson's relief the Coroner, in his summing up, ruled out any mention of manslaughter, which suggests that, despite local feeling, pressure had been applied from above, and the jury meekly returned a verdict of accidental death. Their further comments on the weakness of the bridge, coupled with the reckless act of piling 20 tons or more of ballast on each of the spans, might well have justified a manslaughter charge, but Stephenson had powerful friends and the Board of Trade did not see fit to pursue the matter. Among those friends was George Hudson, the railway king himself, then at the height of his powers, and he relied a good deal on both Stephensons, regarding George as a personal friend as well as a business partner.

A general election was due shortly and Hudson, having secured his own return as MP for Sunderland by devious means, concerned himself with the election of friends and allies at York and Whitby. With Robert Stephenson's approval, Hudson put his name forward as the Tory candidate for Whitby. The original candidate, Maj. Beresford, was induced to take himself off to a safe seat in Essex, and Stephenson was returned unopposed. Not unfairly, he was regarded as 'the nominee of Mr Hudson' as the 'Yorkshireman' chose to declare. The election came shortly after the inquest at Chester, and any threat of possible prosecution would have scuppered Hudson's ambitions. Similarly George Carr Glyn, chairman of the CHR and also Hudson's banker, would not have wished to see his chief engineer in the dock let alone in prison.

The Dee Bridge was rebuilt and strengthened by additional cast-iron deck panels, designed by Thomas Gooch. These formed a very flat tied arch with the original girders,

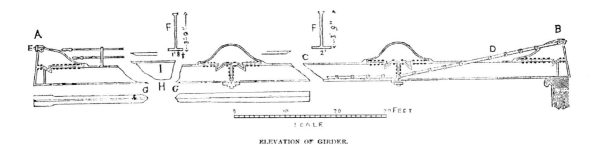

ELEVATION OF GIRDER.

The broken girder of the Dee Bridge. The original point of failure was at C but it also failed in compression at H during the collapse.

which were relieved of much of the weight of traffic. In this form the bridge lasted until completely reconstructed in 1870-1871 with wrought-iron girders. This was not to be the end of the story, for while the original girders were being tested during the rebuilding, another girder failed at less than the rated load. Stephenson had instructed that on no account were the girders to be loaded to excess, and he was both furious and embarrassed when, on 8 September, he had to explain the mishap to the directors. Said Stephenson: 'I attach no importance to the result of the experiment, it does not in any way alter the mode in which I had proposed to add to the strength of this bridge which is now in progress and considerably advanced.'

Even then, on 25 March 1848, *The Builder* reported that one of the original girders had been cracked by a workman driving in a pin with a four-pound hammer, leading, as might be expected to much consternation and yet another new girder. Little wonder that Locke refused to contemplate the use of cast iron.

Despite his problems at Chester, Stephenson's masterly system of delegation allowed work on the tubular bridges to proceed as fast as funds permitted, and Fairbairn, with the assistance of Clark on site, ensured that the work proceeded satisfactorily. However, the fact that a bridge approved by the most eminent engineer in the country (the coroner's description) should be found so seriously wanting caused ripples in Government circles. Even then, safety on the railways was a contentious issue, and not for the first time were the companies accused by the public of putting shareholder interests above those of passengers. A Royal Commission was appointed to examine the whole field of the application of iron to railway structures.

The Royal Commission of 1847 reported early in 1849 after making most extensive enquiries and undertaking valuable experimental work. Various ironmasters and engineers gave evidence and among the latter there was a wide divergence of views. Fairbairn was of the opinion that cast iron was a treacherous material, and Locke stated that he would never use it for girders. Many of the older generation of engineers were less critical and favoured it for arches where the metal was never under tension. Stephenson was clearly a wiser man and stated that he would not use cast-iron girders for spans over 40ft, but Brunel preferred to limit himself to 35ft. Grissell, who was an iron-founder rather than an engineer, was prepared to cast girders in one piece up to 60ft long. No one now had a good word to say of trussed girders and the final view of the Commissioners was that to attempt to combine two interacting systems of support was to be avoided. No more trussed girders were built for railways. Unfortunately, although wrought iron was coming into wider use, the Commission gave it insufficient attention. Experiments carried out at Portsmouth Dockyard by Capts James and Galton did, however, establish that wrought iron should not be loaded beyond one third of its breaking load for fear of fatigue leading to premature failure. They also concluded that a factor of safety of six should be applied to cast-iron bridges in general.

Samuel Smiles made no mention of the Dee Bridge disaster in his biography of the Stephensons. He was not one to allow inconvenient facts to spoil a good story. Towards the end of his life Stephenson had come to terms with the events of ten years earlier, and he informed Smiles:

The last trussed cast iron girder bridge to remain in service carries the Cromford Canal over the Derby to Matlock railway. This is the classic design but the extra depth of the sides of the trough allows a more efficient use of the sloping tendons.

> *The objection to this girder is common to all girders in which two independent systems are attempted to be blended and as a general principle, all such arrangements should be avoided. It is useless to say more on this form of girder as since the adoption of wrought iron for girders they have been entirely superseded ; they were designed when no other means existed of obtaining iron girders of great span. And the melancholy accident which occurred at Chester is the only existing instance of their failure.*

Not entirely true, for the early bridge at Tottenham had suffered a broken girder, but the wrought iron trussing held and trains continued to use the bridge until the break was discovered and the girder replaced.

The trussed girder bridge at Stockton-on-Tees, which replaced Capt. Samuel Brown's unfortunate suspension bridge, was the last to be rebuilt. For many years it was propped up from below, and being on a mineral line did not attract the attention of the Board of Trade. It was finally replaced in 1907, the last of its type. The only relic of trussed girders appears to be two cast-iron girder sections without the trussing now acting as a parapet girder on an underbridge just outside Halifax Station in Yorkshire. One genuine trussed cast-iron girder bridge still exists in the form of an aqueduct where the Cromford Canal crosses the railway from Derby to Matlock. This can be attributed to Thomas Gooch, who was engineer on the line. Along with the canal, it is now classed as an ancient monument.

1. An imaginary scene painted by the well-known portrait painter, John Lucas, from individual sketches, and notable for the omission of Fairbairn, Hodgkinson and Francis Thompson, while including Locke and Brunel as guests. While somewhat idealised it is an important record.

Standing, from left to right:

Capt. Constantine Moorsom RN	Resident Director of the Chester & Holyhead Railway Co.
Latimer Clark	Assistant to his elder brother Edwin.
Edwin Clark	Resident Engineer for the tubes at Britannia.
Frank Forster	Resident Engineer for the line from Conwy to Holyhead, including the Britannia Bridge.
George Parker Bidder	Stephenson's closest associate but he played no part in the Chester & Holyhead Railway.
John Hemingway	Master mason in a consortium with Nowell & Pearson at Britannia.
Capt. Christopher Claxton RN	A close associate of Brunel and in charge of floating out the tubes at Conwy and Britannia.
Alexander McKenzie Ross	Resident Engineer for the line from Chester to Conwy and all operations on the Conwy Bridge after Fairbairn left in 1848.

Seated, from left to right:

Robert Stephenson	Engineer-in-Chief.
Charles Heard Wild	Resident Engineer for bridges and stations.
Joseph Locke	A visiting guest, unconnected with the bridges.
Isambard Kingdom Brunel	Also a visiting friend of Stephenson, but playing little direct part in the bridges.

Frank Forster

George Parker Bidder

Capt. Christopher Claxton RN

Alexander McKenzie Ross

Charles Heard Wild

John Hemingway

Capt. Constantine Moorsom RN

Latimer Clark

Edwin Clark

2. Crymlyn Viaduct was built in 1857 to cross the Ebbw Valley in South Wales and was the second major bridge in Britain to use the Warren girder. At the time of building it was the highest railway viaduct in the world. The line closed in 1964 and corrosion forced its demolition in 1967.

3. Walnut Tree Viaduct of 1901, north of Cardiff, shows the N truss in its heyday. Similar viaducts were built by the Barry Railway at Llanbradach and Penyrheol, but both were demolished in 1937 when the line closed. The short section over Walnut Tree Viaduct remained in use until 1967 and the girders were removed in 1969.

4. A fine view of the Britannia Bridge in sunlight, taken from Anglesey, some years before its destruction by fire in 1970. The taper on the tubes from the Britannia tower to the abutments is scarcely visible. The bridge appears, generally, as it did when it was built a century before.

5. St Pinnock Viaduct, Cornwall – at 151ft it is the highest of Brunel's timber viaducts in Cornwall. Built in 1859, the viaduct was rebuilt in 1882 using iron N trusses for the first time on a main line, while retaining the original stone piers.

6. The Bull Bridge Aqueduct. A lithograph by Samuel Russell showing the fine stone aqueduct built by Alexander M. Ross to carry the Cromford Canal over the newly built North Midland Railway. The iron trough used to keep the canal open is hidden by the masonry. The road passes through an original arch.

7. Hunderton Bridge, a fine example of a cast-iron arch bridge over the River Wye at Hereford, although it no longer carries trains. It replaced an earlier bridge of 1854.

8. Glen Falloch Viaduct on the West Highland Railway 1892: span 118ft, height 144ft. A typical application of the widely used double triangular or X truss. The engineers were Formans & McCall.

9. Brunel's remarkable bridge across the River Wye at Chepstow had a main span of 300ft. It was opened on 19 July 1852 and replaced in November 1962 by a welded Warren girder. Both bridges were built in the same Chepstow shipyard of Fairfield Engineering.

10. Fairbairn's box girder viaduct at Dinting Vale, which replaced earlier timber arches in 1860. The additional brick piers that were added in 1918 by the Great Central Railway are clearly visible and have ruined its appearance. The uneven spacing was forced by ground obstructions.

11. The former viaduct at Staithes, North Yorkshire, showing the replacement plate girders and additional horizontal bracing between the piers.

12. Abraham Darby's iron bridge across the River Severn, the first large iron bridge, built in 1779 to the design of T.F. Pritchard, a Shrewsbury architect.

13. A rare lenticular truss bridge built by Sir John Fowler on his Scottish Highland estate.

14. Conwy – preparation for lifting the western tube, with the castle in the background.

15. Floating the second Conwy tube. Lithograph by George Hawkins.

16. The Conwy Bridge completed, hiding Telford's suspension road bridge of 1826, and showing the close proximity of the ancient castle dating from about 1284.

17. The towers and abutments at Menai under construction. Stone for the central Britannia tower was unloaded directly from ships in the Strait.

18. The top cells under construction at Menai, with the stonework of the towers rising in the background. In practice the top plates were mostly 12ft long, which explains the problems of access for riveting noted by Sir Francis Head.

19. Two of the Britannia tubes under construction on the massive timber decking. The vast amount of timber used must have laid waste to several small forests.

20. The Britannia tower nearing completion. In the foreground are the crane and wharf for unloading stone on the Anglesey shore. Lithograph by G. Hawkins.

21. Floating out the first Caernarfon tube with the first Anglesey tube already raised into position. There was only one set of lifting gear available.

22. The Britannia Bridge at the time of its completion. A tinted lithograph by George Hawkins.

23. William Fairbairn's box girder bridge over the Spey.

24. Chester Station. The buildings were designed by Francis Thompson and the train shed roof is attributed to Charles Heard Wild.

25. The Crymlyn Viaduct.

26. The Forth Bridge of 1890 displays the double triangular, or X, truss at its zenith. It was designed by Benjamin Baker and Allan Duncan Stewart.

27. The Warren girder in the twenty-first century. This structure features the minimalist truss; still a widely used design 150 years after its original patent.

28. Belah Viaduct on the line from Darlington to Penrith. The first major use of the X truss promoted by R.H. Bow. The engineer was Thomas Bouch and the contractors were Gilkes, Wilson & Co. of Middlesbrough.

29. The Torksey Viaduct, built in 1849 by John Fowler and William Fairbairn to cross the Trent in Lincolnshire. There are two box girder spans of 130ft each. The bridge was widened and central Pratt trusses inserted by the Great Central Railway in 1897.

Nine

The Britannia Bridge

Clark's promotion to resident engineer on the Welsh bridges after Fairbairn's resignation was, perhaps, the most remarkable appointment in the history of engineering. For one so inexperienced to rise so high and so fast demonstrated Stephenson's considerable capacity for judicious delegation, and for choosing subordinates on whose skill and loyalty he could rely while at the same allowing them freedom to develop their talents – Brunel's weakness was Stephenson's strength. It must be remembered, though, that in Forster and Ross, and their team of assistants, there were many experienced engineers, and in the day-to-day management of the contracts, Clark was a supernumerary with no well-defined functions except to act as ears and eyes for Stephenson.

How the Britannia Bridge was to be erected still remained unresolved. The first proposal – to assemble the tubes on a platform suspended from chains – was clearly impracticable. Stephenson then suggested that the tubes should be constructed on the land approaches, and rolled out over the suspended platform, which had been pre-loaded with wagons piled with pig iron. As the tube advanced, the weights would be withdrawn, thus maintaining a constant level. This was fine in theory but hardly a practical proposition. Fairbairn had suggested a double cantilever system, working out from piers, as had been proposed previously for the arches, but on mature reflection this was felt to be too dangerous in high winds.

In his book Clark claimed that, while waiting on Crewe Station, he had watched a large water tank being raised into position with screw-jacks while the brickwork was built up beneath it as it rose. He suggested a similar method might be employed for raising the bridge tubes. William Evans, the contractor at Conwy, took up this proposal with enthusiasm and he is credited with the idea of building the tubes on staging at the waterside and floating them into position. He had the courage of his convictions and undertook full responsibility for the floating and lifting of both the Conwy tubes. At Menai it was decided that the land spans should be assembled on staging in their final position, and the main tubes fabricated on platforms along the shoreline. Floating out would be hazardous for, even in the best of weather, tides on the Strait run fiercely, and there is only a very short period of slack water at high tide. Even so, with the particular conditions at Menai, no other method seemed feasible. There remained the small problem of lifting the tubes 100ft in the air.

A Mr J. Faulding, writing to *The Times*, suggested that the tubes might be raised stage by stage by leaving the pontoons under the tube, adding scaffolding after each tide, and lifting 15ft at a time on successive high tides. Another proposal was to use a weighted pontoon attached to the tube by ropes passing over the tower. Both proposals were vetoed as being dangerous and generally impracticable. Even so, some still argued that chains might be

The proposal for raising the Britannia tubes by tidal power was neither practical nor safe.

needed to assist in the lifting. Fairbairn strongly disagreed, placing his faith in a system which he devised, using hydraulic jacks (or presses as was the customary name at the time).

It was in mid-July 1846 that Fairbairn put these proposals to Stephenson, who was then deeply involved in parliamentary work in the House of Lords for three railway companies, while at the same time resisting intense pressure from his doctor for him to rest. The strain of his enormous workload was starting to undermine a constitution that he had driven unmercifully as a young man. In spite of some misgivings, Stephenson so far accepted the scheme that, a month later, he was urging Fairbairn to proceed with the staging and workshops for the building of the tubes. At the same time, Fairbairn was investigating the supply of special lifting chains and his drawing office in Manchester, where he employed a dozen draughtsmen, was engaged on the working drawings for the tubes under the supervision of Mr Blair. Blair was supervised in his turn by the indefatigable Edwin Clark, or so Clark would have us believe.

Drawings for the workshops had already been put in hand in mid-May, and were completed within a month. Fairbairn wasted no time, and in less than four months the shores at Menai were hidden under a massive timber staging, $3\frac{1}{4}$ acres in extent, together with extensive workshops, which included the latest tools and machinery such as Garforth's steam riveting machine, and steam driven rolls for flattening the plates. Plates were far from true when received from the rolling mills. At Conwy, where Evans had far fewer plates to handle, this operation had to be carried out in the traditional manner with 40lb sledgehammers on a cast-iron stretching block. With an eye to economy, discarded tubes from the Millwall tests were adapted as chimneys for some of the rivet heating furnaces at Menai, forty-eight in all.

Disputes over Priority for the Cellular Concept

Relations with Hodgkinson were becoming ever more strained as he was now claiming priority for the idea of cellular tops. Matters came to a head at a meeting of the British Association at Southampton in September 1846, where both he and Fairbairn presented papers, and Hodgkinson publicly repeated his claim. To add to the confusion, Stephenson too, in a letter to Fairbairn in late October, claimed that he had developed a cellular construction for a bridge at Ware some years earlier. He wrote: 'It was I believe a counterpart of the proposed top of the Britannia Bridge.'

When challenged by Fairbairn, Stephenson produced a drawing of a built-up wrought-iron beam bearing no resemblance to any form of cell, but he argued that a series of beams side by side formed virtual cells. This did not prevent Stephenson and Clark from repeating the claim later, although it was admitted that the apocryphal design for Ware was never built. Fairbairn countered with a copy of a letter outlining the cellular concept, written to Stephenson on the same day that Hodgkinson had first visited Millwall, and his three senior foremen at Millwall gave written statements supporting his claim to priority. By then the seeds of dissent had been well and truly sown.

Towards the end of September 1846 Stephenson was obliged to go abroad for six weeks, and when he returned in early November the contract drawings had been completed in Fairbairn's drawing office and had been signed by Fairbairn himself. These drawings still exist. On his return the drawings were presented to Stephenson for his approval in order that the tubes might go out to tender without further delay. Regardless of a mere seven months' experience and having no training in drawing office work, Clark was later to claim in his book that he had personally completed the drawings. Stephenson, deeply involved in so many other projects and in poor health, was able to devote little time to the bridges, and he became very concerned that Fairbairn was stealing his thunder. Tensions between the two men started to build up and would grow over the coming months.

With the design of the tubes finalised, Fairbairn turned his attention to the supplies of iron. Provisional orders had already been placed with a number of ironmasters since the mass production of wrought iron was still at an early stage of development and a large part of the available output was absorbed by the rapidly expending shipbuilding industry. In addition, there were problems over quality and few works could roll the width of plate needed for the bottom cells. In total some 12,000 tons of good quality iron would be required. Priority was given to the Conwy tubes to allow opening of the line as far a Bangor and, by February of 1847, enough iron had been received for Evans to start punching plates. Meanwhile a start on the Britannia tubes was delayed but, as the company was facing one of its recurring shortages of capital, this breathing space may not have been unwelcome.

Contracts for the Tubes are Awarded

The contract for the first Britannia tube was awarded to Garforth of Dukinfield, but it had been expected that Fairbairn's Millwall yard and Ditchburn & Mare of Blackwall would share the fabrication of the remaining seven Menai tubes. Fairbairn's appointment as a salaried engineer now involved a conflict of interest. The matter was smoothed over, but at a meeting of the finance committee in January 1847 some strong criticisms were voiced concerning the continuing outlay on Hogkinson's experiments, which appeared to be getting nowhere despite the full-time employment of six or seven of Fairbairn's men. Regardless of their differences, Hodgkinson had continued to enjoy the facilities of the Manchester works. The cost had now risen to over £6,000, double that originally approved, and Stephenson admitted that it was time to call a halt. For his part, Fairbairn complained that Hodgkinson would not disclose the purpose of his experiments, which appeared to have no useful purpose except satisfying Hodgkinson's scientific curiosity. In fact he undertook some very useful work which he reported in detail to the 1847 Royal Commission, which later published it.

One practical outcome seems to have been a demonstration that cast-iron tops could be used in place of wrought-iron cells. This information Hodgkinson conveyed to Stephenson in a letter at the end of February 1847 and Stephenson commended to Fairbairn the use of cast-iron tops for box girder bridges, although accepting that the tubular bridges could not be modified at such a late stage. It was also at this juncture that, with Fairbairn's approval, the top cells were reduced to a single row and increased in size to permit easier access for riveting and painting. It is unclear why a double layer of cells had been introduced into the design, since it greatly complicated construction. Stephenson had some smaller box girder bridges built with cast-iron tops, although after constructing four the idea was abandoned. These will be described in a later chapter.

Lifting Machinery for the Tubes

While agreement had been reached on floating out the tubes, the machinery for lifting them was still under consideration, and once again it fell to Fairbairn to devise the means. Design work started at the end of January 1847 and Fairbairn was able to report two months later that the drawings had been completed and that enquiries were being made regarding the hydraulic presses. The proposed scheme involved massive cast-iron cross girders carrying the presses and situated near the tops of the towers above the highest point of lifting. In turn, the presses had a crosshead carrying chains from which the tubes would be suspended. The presses were to have a stroke of 6ft so that the full lift would be carried out in a number of stages, the masonry being built up closely under the ends of the tube while each stage was completed. At Conwy, because the tubes were lighter, a single press at each end of the tube was sufficient but at Britannia, where a much greater weight was involved, the smaller presses from Conwy would be used as a pair at one end and a third, and proportionately larger, press at the other. One of the crosshead castings at Conwy developed cracks while lifting was under way, but fortunately it held until the lift was completed. In the light of this potentially dangerous weakness, fabricated wrought iron from components had to be adopted for the conditions at Menai.

The chains were of a newly patented type, where the end eyes were rolled in one piece with the link, instead of being welded on, as had been the custom previously, resulting in a far more reliable product. Fairbairn approached the patentee, Thomas Howard, of Howard & Ravenhill at the King & Queen Ironworks, Rotherhithe, and an order was placed. Each link was 7in wide and 1in thick, with 6ft between the centres of the eyes. Great precision was necessary so that each link would bear its fair share of the load when coupled in sets.

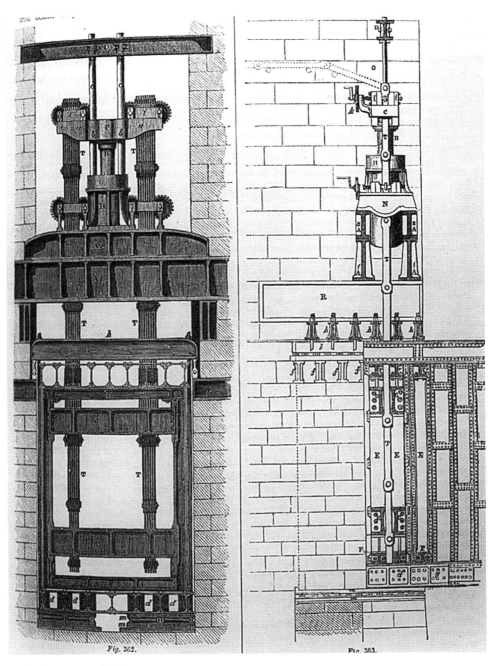

Fig. 362.   Fig. 363.

Hydraulic press and lifting gear.

The pumps and hydraulic presses were supplied by Easton & Amos of Southwark, who specialised in extrusion presses for seamless lead pipes. Each pump was driven by a 40hp steam engine, and could operate at up to 2 tons per square inch. The pressure pipes were of $\frac{1}{2}$in bore with $\frac{1}{4}$in walls. The large cylinder proved unsatisfactory due to an initial problem with a porous casting. The pressure was such that water was forced through the pores of the casting and as a result the working pressure could not be built up sufficiently. To cure this a very fine-grained iron had to be substituted. This was not to be an end to the problems, for the large single-cylinder cast for use at Menai failed during lifting due to the body breaking away from the base as will be described later. It took six weeks to cast and machine a redesigned cylinder at the Bank Quay Foundry, Warrington, but after that unwelcome delay no further serious faults occurred. The base of the original cylinder can still be seen on a plinth at the site at Menai.

What became of the great press after completion of the lifting of the Britannia tubes is not recorded, but it made a public appearance at the Great Exhibition of 1851, after which it again vanished into obscurity until at the end of 1857, when Brunel was desperate for extra hydraulic power to launch the *Great Eastern* at Millwall. It was dragged from its retirement and added its considerable efforts to those of a motley collection of presses drawn from far and wide. Success followed and by the end of January 1858 the great ship was finally floated. Thereafter the fate of the Britannia press seems to have gone unrecorded.

The Rise of Britannia

By the end of 1846, the staging and workshops at Menai were ready, but priority was given to the Conwy site as limited supplies of iron plates became available. The ironmasters were not slow to combine in raising their prices and this factor contributed much to the final costs being far in excess of the 1845 estimates. In negotiating tender prices for the ironwork, the company undertook to supply the tube builders at £15 per ton, regardless of any changes in the market. The purchasing of the iron was left to Fairbairn to negotiate and tenders were accepted from five suppliers, including the famous Butterley and Coalbrookdale works. The latter got off to a shaky start by having their first delivery of 10 tons of plates condemned by Fairbairn for poor finish.

The original tenders accepted for the fabrication were from Garforth of Dukinfield and a certain Horton of Brierley Hill, but the latter proved to be unequal to the task and was dismissed from the contract with the work being allocated instead to Charles Mare. The six remaining tubes were in the beginning to be shared equally between Fairbairn's shipyard at Millwall and their competitors Ditchburn & Mare.

Once the company had appointed Fairbairn as joint engineer with Stephenson he had become an interested party and his son, Thomas, entered into a private arrangement with Mare for the latter to complete all seven tubes. At the board meeting on 12 May 1847, news of this arrangement was unfavourably received by the directors, who considered that they should have been consulted before so many eggs were placed in one basket. Unpleasant rumours were circulating that Fairbairn had received a handsome commission from Mare for putting this business his way, but these were strongly refuted by Fairbairn and his son.

What galled him more was that his power to sign certificates was removed and given to Clark, deputising for Stephenson. The final position was that Garforth was contracted to build one main tube and Ditchburn & Mare the remaining seven. All cast-iron work was awarded to the Bank Quay Foundry at Warrington at £7 10s (£7.50) per ton.

Charles J. Mare: a Man of Several Parts

In view of the major part played by Charles J. Mare at Menai his story may be of interest. Born in Derbyshire and trained as a solicitor, he entered into a partnership in 1837, at the age of twenty-two, with Thomas Ditchburn, a shipwright. Starting with small river steamers at a yard in Blackwall, they moved on to being accepted on the Admiralty list by 1843. Ditchburn retired in 1846 at the age of forty-five, leaving Mare as sole proprietor. After his successful completion of the Britannia tubes, Mare was well placed to tender for Brunel's great bridge at Saltash, and in January 1853, he was awarded the contract for the ironwork for £162,000 including the seventeen approach spans. The yard flourished and quickly expanded into building ocean-going ships but ran into financial difficulties, to which underpricing of the Saltash bridge may well have contributed. Mare's work, until his financial position deteriorated to a point where the company was forced to take over, received high praise from Brunel. In 1857 Mare's former business was resurrected as the Thames Ironworks & Shipbuilding Co., under the direction of Peter Rolt, Mare's father-in-law, and expanded into structural ironwork, rolling its own wrought iron plate and sections from scrap. Mare went on to other business ventures in the same field, dying in 1905. It has been said of him:

> Mare's various establishments were pretty fair examples of Victorian free enterprise in mid-century. Like most he was a man of several parts. A rich man, a professional man, a man of the world and a man who knew his way around the financial world. He reached great heights and he ended in failure. An interesting man.

Stephenson had good cause to be grateful to Mare for a job well done but no such appreciation was ever expressed publicly.

The first delivery of iron arrived at Menai on 13 June 1847 and, during the following month, the timber staging was finally completed. On 10 August, Clark drove the first rivet under Mare's watchful eye. By 5 May 1849 the first Britannia tube was complete and ready for floating out. It had taken twenty months, having suffered serious delays due to lack of money.

Construction of the tubes presented no special problems, having much in common with the building of a ship's hull. The plates were flattened in a set of cold rolls and the edges dressed. Punching of rivet holes was done in a steam driven machine designed by Garforth, but this was slow, and accurate results depended on the care taken in marking out and the skill of the operators. There is no record of a machine similar to Roberts' multiple punching machine at Conwy being used at Menai despite the far greater number of holes to be punched and resistance to machinery on the part of Mare's men may well have been

The Victoria Bridge, Montréal. Works in progress on the piers.

the reason. Clark would surely have mentioned it, yet he refers only to the Conwy machine, which in any case belonged to William Evans. The use of riveting machines was opposed by the workers at Menai. In practice these machines, although valuable in a boiler shop, required the work to be brought to the machine which severely limited its utility.

Initially, the quality of hand riveting caused some concern and this was attributed to the use of two-pound hammers customary in the shipyards where smaller rivets were in general use. The substitution of four-pound hammers gave much improved results. Like on the keel of a ship the bottom cells were constructed first, the sides were raised up and one layer of top plates laid down. After the cell dividers had been fixed, the top layer of plates was riveted on. This was rather a tricky operation as the 21in internal width of the cells offered little room for a man, let alone a rivet boy who had to put the red hot rivets into place from inside the cells. The Act of 1844 prohibiting the use of boys as chimney sweeps had proved a dead letter for it was ignored by common consent. Let Sir Francis Head take up the story:

> *A tiny rivet boy – we observed one little mite only ten years of age – in clothes profes-sionally worn into holes at the knees and elbows – crawling heel foremost for a considerable distance into one of these flues as a yellow ferret trots into a rabbit hole, is slowly followed by his huge Lord and Master the holder-up, who exactly fits the flue, for the plain and excellent reason that by Mr Stephenson the flue was purposely predestined to be exactly big enough to fit him; and as, buried alive in this receptacle, he can move but very slowly, he requires some time, advancing head foremost, to reach the point at which he is to commence his work…*

He goes on to describe how a boy at a rivet furnace on the ground would throw a red hot rivet some 45ft into the air where it was caught by a colleague on top of the tube who ran with it, crawled up the cell or flue, and inserted the rivet into a waiting hole.

The holder-up quickly raised his heavy sledgehammer to hold the rivet in place, while two riveters on top formed the head, using a cup-shaped swage to give the final shape. Some twelve blows with the hammer followed by eight on the swage were needed for each rivet. Each riveting gang for the bridge required three men and two boys.

On 5 May 1849 the first of the main tubes was at last completed, getting on for almost two years after the first rivet had been driven. Work was proceeding simultaneously on the second tube and, by the end of November 1849, it too was ready for floating out. In April 1848 Stephenson ordered progress on the two remaining main tubes to be slowed down due to increasing financial pressures. The prime cause was the aftermath of the wild excesses of the Railway Mania, and worse was yet to come in the months ahead, but by December 1848 construction of the last two main tubes was making slow but satisfactory progress and work had started on the four side spans. Another six months would pass until the first main tube would be ready for floating out.

Floating out the First Span at Menai

The real test was now to come. The tube had been strengthened internally with cast-iron frames but the risk remained that it might be distorted during handling and lifting. A model of the Strait had been constructed to allow the manoeuvres to be worked out in detail, and it took a further four months to cut away the rock and remove the platform to allow the pontoons to be floated under the tube. Stephenson had been unhappy with the timber pontoons at Conwy, though they had served their purpose and he was taking no chances under the more severe conditions at Menai. He was authorised to order two more to be built of iron, for he reasoned that their resale value would offset the greater first cost. The eight pontoons had a total lifting capacity of 3,200 tons – twice the weight of a tube. Among others, Sir Francis Head chronicled the events in his usual florid style. He was able to watch the proceedings along with other privileged observers, from the top of the second almost completed tube.

The shores of Menai had never before seen such a gathering. Crowds had come by train from Chester and beyond, and every local mode of conveyance was pressed into service to bring sightseers from miles around. It was a Welsh version of Derby Day, with all the fun of the fair supported by every form of portable catering. Flags and bunting were flying, musicians of varying ability were performing and in general the crowd was giving little attention to the serious business that lay ahead. Even the temperance movement seems to have got in on the act, for Sir Francis comments:

> *Numbers of persons with heated faces, standing around small tables allocated in various directions, were intently occupied in quaffing of a beautiful unanalysed pink effervescing mixture, called by its proprietor 'ginger beer'.*

Doubtless the real ale tents were doing even better trade!

The first attempt to float the tube was made on the evening of 19 June when wind and tide were propitious but to the disappointment of the onlookers this had to be cut short when one of the capstans failed and the tube had to be dragged back ignomiously into its dock. These capstans had been set up in strategic positions to control the movements of the pontoons, and Charles Wild had contrived 'cable stoppers' which allowed the massive ropes to be released under full control, something difficult if not dangerous to attempt with a capstan alone. Capt. Claxton was prominent with his speaking-trumpet supervising the sailors, 105 on each pontoon, and directed operations with flag signals. The directors and their guests were accommodated on a stand built on the Anglesey shore.

As the spectators drifted away to whatever overnight shelter they could find, preparations were made for a fresh start the next morning at seven o'clock. Once again, a capstan failed and a further attempt was arranged for the evening tide. As usual the *Illustrated London News* had their man on the spot, and his description of the proceedings was graphic:

About 7.30 p.m. the first perceptible motion, which indicated that the tide was lifting the mass, was observed, and, at Mr Stephenson's desire, the depth of water was ascertained and the exact time noted. In a few minutes the motion was plainly visible, the tube being fairly moved forward some inches. This moment was one of intense interest; the huge bulk gliding as gently and easily forward as if she had been but a small boat. The spectators seemed spell-bound, for no shouts or exclamations were heard, as all watched silently the silent course of the heavily freighted pontoons, The only sounds heard were the shouts from Captain Claxton as he gave directions to 'Let go ropes' to 'haul in faster' and 'broadside on': the tube floated majestically in the middle of the straits. This was no easy task, the tide running strong…

The first Anglesey tube has been floated out and is lying at the base of the towers while the lifting gear is being assembled. This picture can be dated as being between 20 June and 10 August 1849, when lifting first started.

A view of the staging on the Anglesey side with both short land tubes half completed. The massive timber staging had to carry a load exceeding 1,300 tons.

At 8.35 p.m. the tube was nearing the Anglesey pier, and at this moment the expectation of the spectators was greatly increased, as the tube was so near its destination. Soon all fears were dispelled as the Anglesey end of the tube passed beyond the pier, and then the Britannia pier end neared its appointed spot and was instantly drawn back close to the pier, so as to rest on the bearing intended for it. There was then a pause for a few minutes while waiting for the tide to turn; and when that took place the huge bulk floated gently into its place on the Anglesey pier – rested on the bearing there and was instantly made fast so that it could not move again. The cheering, until then subdued, was loud and hearty.

It was not in fact so smooth a process as the reporter suggests and this time the coils of rope became jammed on the Llanfair capstan, dragging the whole machine out of the ground and knocking down men despite their frantic efforts. Disaster was very close when foreman Charles Rolfe who was in charge called on the spectators to assist by grasping the spare rope. A crowd of men, women and even children seized the rope and managed to restrain the movement of the tube. It was two hours before the tube rested securely beneath the towers, by which time the tide had gained force and there was difficulty in recovering the pontoons. As darkness fell there was a vast sense of relief all round, but the perils of lifting still lay ahead.

There were delays and, whether or not the Admiralty liked it, one channel would remain blocked for nearly eight weeks. On 22 June Stephenson laid the last stone in the Britannia tower. During the following weeks the lifting presses, two from Conwy and one new and larger one in the Anglesey tower, were installed together with the new wrought-iron crossheads and the lifting chains. First attempts to lift the tube were abortive, for the new cylinder leaked too badly to allow pressure to build up. Stephenson reported to the company secretary on 7 August that a new cylinder might be required, involving a delay of up to eight weeks. The hydraulic pump manufacturer, Mr Amos, was on site and, using some secret of the trade, succeeded in curing the leakage, for on 10 August lifting was able to start again.

As a wise precaution Stephenson had ordered brickwork to be built under the ends of the tube as it rose. This prevented a major catastrophe when, on 17 August, and with the tube raised 24ft, the large Anglesey cylinder cracked at its base allowing the tube to fall about 9in on to the timber packing below. A sailor was killed; Clark and his brother had a narrow escape and the top cells were damaged. In six weeks a new redesigned cylinder arrived from Warrington and lifting recommenced on 1 October, the tube reaching its full height on the 13th. By 10 November the junction piece and the short Anglesey land span had been riveted on, and the tubes lowered on to the expansion rollers. This was not to be an end to the mishaps for on 20 November, when lowering the large cylinder for transfer to the Caernarfon tower, the cylinder broke free and fell into the water. Another unfortunate sailor was killed and three men were injured, but the cylinder itself was recovered from the water undamaged.

In late November Stephenson arrived for the floating of the second tube. Despite minor problems the tube was floated out on 4 December and deposited just above high water level, with its safe arrival saluted by a battery of cannon. Five weeks later, on 7 January 1850, after having its end in the Caernarfon tower lifted to allow completion of the Britannia junction, it was bedded in on its rollers. On 4 March the first line of tube was completed and the permanent way, of Brunel's GWR-type bridge rail, was laid without chairs on longitudinal timbers. A continuous line of rails now ran from Holyhead to

Capt. John Lintorn Arabin Simmons RE (1821-1903) was Inspector of Railways, 1847-1853, and Secretary of the Railway Department of the Board of Trade, 1851-1853. This photograph was taken in 1855 while he was serving with the Turkish Army in the Crimea at the siege of Sevastopol.

London and other parts, and the company's steamers completed the journey to Kingstown (Dun Laoghaire). From there, Ireland's first railway, engineered and completed by Charles Blacker Vignoles in 1834, sped the weary travellers to the heart of Dublin where rest and refreshment awaited.

Captain Simmons and the Board of Trade Report

The first line of tubes had been completed end to end and it was a great day for all concerned. Almost four years and nine months had passed since the Bill had first been presented to Parliament back in May 1845. The following day Stephenson drove the final rivet at a small ceremony and Mare applied the finishing touches. The rivet head was painted white and so it remained for the next century, no doubt touched up from time to time, until the Centenary ceremonies in March 1950 when the inscription was renewed. After the disastrous fire of 1970 only a few flakes of paint remained but the section was cut out during the demolition and now lies in the National Railway Museum whence it was recently sent on loan to a 'Victorian Vision' exhibition at the V&A Museum.

The 5 March 1850 started off auspiciously with glorious weather and at 6.30 a.m. a train hauled by three locomotives left Bangor, with Stephenson driving the leading engine across the bridge. Twenty-one wagons of coal made up a total load of about 300 tons. At noon, heralded by cannon fire, the last rivet was driven in by Stephenson with Mare in attendance. To the rousing tones of 'Rule Britannia', another train, made up of forty-five coal wagons and carriages for 700 people, weighing altogether some 500 tons, crossed the bridge to Anglesey. After detaching the coal wagons the train proceeded to Holyhead where a sumptuous repast was served at the Royal Hotel, followed by the usual fulsome and well-lubricated speeches. Unfortunately this happy event coincided with a worsening of the financial situation and the mood of the directors at their meeting shortly afterwards was somewhat sombre. Nonetheless, after receiving reassurances from an equally sombre Capt. Moorsom, they resolved to press ahead with completion of the second line of tubes.

The formal inspection of the first line of tubes took place on 15 March and Capt. Simmons RE was sent to do his duty. After a rather bruising encounter at the Dee Bridge inquest, where Simmons among others had demolished Stephenson's defence that the accident had been caused by a derailment, the two men were doubtless wary of one another. In his report, Capt. Simmons accepted Stephenson's assurance that the use of the continuity had reduced the maximum stress in the iron from 5.15 tons per square inch to 3 tons per square inch. These figures appear not to be corroborated in Clark's book but, verging on the optimistic, they are for an unloaded tube. A full working load would have seen them increased by about thirty per cent. As Simmons reported: '...having full reliance in the care and skill displayed in constructing this immense tube, I fell assured that every confidence may be placed in the security of the structure...'

The Dee Bridge failure three years earlier had established the principle that the company and its engineer were ultimately responsible for the safety of their structures. Simmons was therefore in a stronger position than Maj.-Gen. Pasley had been at Chester and he contented himself with checking the deflection produced by a modest train of coal wagons weighing 228 tons rather then the 460 tons which each span was designed to carry. He could only report on what was visible and he had good cause to be impressed with what he saw. The first public train service ran on 18 March 1850.

Initially, points were provided at each end of the tube and single line working was controlled by a pilot-man who rode on every train to cross the bridge. If there was no balancing return service he had to struggle through the sulphurous gloom of the tube but a thoughtful designer had provided a tiny glass porthole at intervals to light his way.

Stephenson had been concerned from the outset regarding the effect any high winds might have on whatever bridge design was chosen. The deck of Telford's bridge had been severely damaged in a storm in January 1839. It was the reduced wind loading on a circular or elliptical tube which he had to offset against the superior strength of a rectangular one. To satisfy himself he set Clark to work to compute the wind load at a pressure of 20lb per square foot on the side of the tube. Clark concluded that the maximum stress that this would cause in the iron would be about half a ton per square inch. Unusually, the natural period of vibration of the bridge when struck by a gust of wind was also assessed and found to be sixty-seven cycles per minute, or 1.117Hz.

The second line of tubes was completed successfully although the same risks had to be faced during floating out, and once again there were problems with the fouling of lines. Brunel was again in attendance, offering Stephenson moral support as an enormous crowd had again turned up to watch the spectacle. The third tube was floated on 19 June 1850 and the lift completed by 11 July. The final main tube was floated on 25 July and was in position by 16 August. The side tubes were already in place on their scaffolding and all that remained was to complete the junction pieces. By 19 October, the second complete tube was ready for inspection and again Capt. Simmons was able to report favourably.

At this period there was much controversy over the effects of a moving load. Did it, as some argued, reduce the deflection the faster it went, or did it make any difference at all? There was an awkward minority who insisted that the vibration and impact of a moving load increased the stresses in the structure and needed to be taken into account. In the hope of resolving this conflict of opinion, which in fact was to take another eighty years, Capt. Simmons, who happened to belong to the awkward squad, was permitted to carry out a series of trials on the Sunday before the bridge first opened. Unfortunately, it depended on a water level to check the deflection of the tubes. Not the most precise of instruments even under static conditions, it was completely useless for the purpose in hand, having too sluggish a response. Consequently, the lack of results apparently confirmed the views of the majority, the faster the better party, and the Captain was taken to task by the press for expressing views contrary to natural law. Having, as the pundits observed, wasted the Sabbath, the trains were able to start running on the following Monday.

In practice, the inertia of the massive tubes was so great that the small locomotives of the day would have had little effect, but a century later, with locomotives of four or five times the weight, impact loading was to become a more serious concern. It was a shame that Simmons, who was acting with the best of intentions and who, moreover, would ultimately be proved correct, should have met with so much criticism and derision. He had chosen to challenge the views of the engineering establishment, led by Stephenson, and those who supported his theories were forced to keep their heads down or suffer similar criticism. Yet they had powerful support from the 1847 Royal Commission tests though everybody who was anybody in the profession chose to ignore them. To quote from *Tomlinson's Cyclopaedia of the Arts*:

> *Engineers have generally supposed that the deflection caused by passing a weight at a high velocity over a girder is less than the deflection which would be produced by the same weight at rest; and even when they have observed an increase, they have attributed it solely to the jerks of the engine or train, produced by passing over inequalities at the junction of the rails, or other similar causes.*

The Royal Commission had been very thorough in its inquiries, and one of these was intended to settle the controversy over the effects of a moving load. A series of tests were carried out on two bridges over roads, by measuring the deflections caused by a locomotive at rest in the centre of the span and in motion at various speeds. Their apparatus was of the simplest, consisting of a pencil fixed in the middle of the span and a piece of paper on a board rigidly supported from the road below. As the bridge flexed, so the pencil moved over the paper. It was convincingly demonstrated that a fast moving locomotive would increase the deflection by up to nearly one third compared with the same locomotive at rest. Thus, the locomotive which weighed 33 tons at rest would exert a force of 43.4 tons on the bridge when travelling at 73ft per second or 66mph. Though published in May 1849 these particular findings provoked absolutely no response from anybody in the engineering establishment in Westminster. Ignorance was bliss for the best part of another fifty years!

In 1848 little attempt was made to balance the reciprocating forces caused by the pistons and motion of a locomotive. Since with the small locomotives in current use the vertical component of these forces was not great, the impact effect on the track was not excessive and generally ignored. When a few years later the standard of horizontal balancing was improved, it led to much smoother running but at the price of increased pounding of tracks and bridges due to oversize balance weights. The years passed and increasing damage from unbalanced vertical forces continued to be ignored. One result was that bridges, designed on the basis of static load, were by the turn of the century, when British engineers at last woke up to the situation, found to be woefully weak. A spate of expensive bridge strengthening or replacements ensued.

It would be unjust to tar all bridge designers with the same brush. When Joseph Locke commissioned two trussed bowstring arch bridges from Fox, Henderson & Co. in 1848 for use on the Blackwall Extension Railway, the designer, E.A. Cowper, had the trusses tested with 2 tons per foot run to accommodate the almost standard 1 ton per foot loading of the period, together with a further ton for impact loads and vibration. He was a man far ahead of his time – and there were doubtless others. How differently bridge design might have evolved had the majority taken notice of the incontrovertible evidence given by the Royal Commission tests! Unfortunately, in this as in other matters, the majority blindly followed the Stephenson line. Possibly they thought it professional suicide to differ.

The Britannia Bridge in Service

For months after the opening of the line through to Holyhead, inertia of another kind was exhibited by the Post Office juggernaut. According to the *Illustrated London News*:

> *The full benefit of the change will not, however, be experienced until the forms of Government routine have had time to come into operation. In the meantime the* [mail] *bags will continue to be taken out of the train at Bangor, and conveyed round in a cart to Llanfair, where the train will await their arrival.*

It would appear that, throughout its life, no speed limit was in force on the bridge itself, but the sharp curvature on the approaches resulted in limits which had the same effect. In 1857 the LNWR instructed drivers to shut off steam when approaching the bridge, though this did not prevent a derailment not long after which seems to have escaped the attention of the Inspectorate. The LMS imposed a limit of 55mph on the Llanfair curve and 35mph on the Caernarfon side and, by 1948, the Llanfair side too was restricted to 35mph.

Apart from the clearing up and the sale of surplus materials, there remained the matter of roofing the tubes to avoid corrosion and false economy prevailed. Stephenson had been criticised for his apparent extravagance in using corrugated iron at Conwy. In this case he was for some reason not consulted, and Clark, who had already left the Company for greener pastures, advised the use of wood and paper as an economy measure. Paper presumably being what is now called roofing felt. Later upgraded to tarred canvas on wooden boards, it was this highly combustible structure which would promote the rapid spread of the fire which engulfed the tubes in May 1970.

In the two and a half years following Fairbairn's abrupt resignation, Stephenson had been under great pressure. Fairbairn's self confidence had complemented Stephenson's more cautious and less sanguine nature. On his own, and even with the support of Bidder and a trusted staff, Stephenson was to suffer his moments of black doubts, and the strain told on him. Beset by chronic health problems he increasingly turned for relief to alcohol and drugs, to the dismay of his friends and to the further detriment of his health and at only forty-seven years of age he was already past his prime. Quite apart from the Welsh bridges, he was at the same time deeply involved in two trunk lines, the Newcastle & Darlington and the Newcastle & Berwick, which formed the last two links in a chain of companies between London and Edinburgh. The High Level Bridge at Newcastle and the Royal Border Bridge over the Tweed were major undertakings in their own right. The resident engineer, Thomas Elliott Harrison (1808-1888), bore the brunt of the work, with Stephenson himself, as he publicly confessed, merely exercising overall supervision.

At the end of August 1850, Stephenson was offered a knighthood by the Home Secretary, Sir George Grey, at the command of Queen Victoria, but he declined the honour, just as Fairbairn was to do eleven years later. They both justifiably felt that knighthoods were too often given to time servers, or in return for political activities, rather than to those who had rendered genuine public service. Some years before, at his wife's insistence, Stephenson had adopted a coat of arms, derived by some inventive herald from a distant Stephenson of Scottish origins but he himself had never liked or ever used this pretentious emblem. A silly picture, as he described it.

A request from the directors that the Britannia Bridge should be formally opened by the Prince of Wales, then a boy of eight, was refused by the Prince Consort, but in October 1852 the Queen's carriage was drawn through the bridge by a team of workmen during a royal visit to North Wales. Prince Albert and Edward, the young Prince of Wales, accompanied by Stephenson, walked over the top of the tubes, presumably on Clark's wood and paper roof.

Other Tubular Bridges

In 1845 wrought-iron railway bridges of any size were almost unheard of, but within five years the Conwy and Britannia bridges had established wrought iron as the supreme material for long spans. The opening of James Barton's Boyne Viaduct in Ireland in 1855, sometimes regarded as the first scientifically designed truss bridge, saw the open web girder triumphant over the immensely heavy solid plate sides of the train-sized tubular bridges. In 1845, faced with a desperate situation and no precedent to guide him, Stephenson had fortuitously conceived the tubular form of beam, albeit with suspension chains. His doubts as to whether or not such a beam might be self-supporting were finally laid to rest only at Fairbairn's insistence.

Had structural knowledge been further advanced the tubular concept might have been refined, but when that became possible around 1856, the development of open web girders had already rendered the tubular concept obsolescent. Consequently, in spite of his advocacy, Stephenson only built five more tubular bridges and, in the case of his three Egyptian bridges, the rails were carried on top of the tubes rather than through them. However, it is unlikely that Stephenson was much involved with the latter, as the design is attributed to his cousin, George Robert Stephenson, though his assistant B.P. Stockman attended to all the calculations and detailing.

All the development work that had gone into the bridges was not lost. It had long been recognised that the hull of a ship acted as a beam and was subjected to far greater abuse than any railway bridge. The work done by the eminent naval architect, John Scott Russell, in the 1830s had established the 'wave line theory' which offered the optimum lines for the hull of a ship, and confirmed what had long been known – that for speed, a long narrow hull was best. In addition, experience had shown that a large ship was more efficient than a small one, and the demand for longer hulls increased to a point where timber construction was ruled out and iron hulls built on the longitudinal system with cross bulkheads, bearing a close similarity to a tubular girder, were introduced. Brunel had experimented with this system with success in his earlier iron ships. Finally, this use of a cellular construction offered the increased stiffness and resistance to torsional strains demanded. Scott Russell paid public tribute to Fairbairn's experimental work which made possible a hull length of 680ft, resulting in a ship with a displacement six times larger than anything then afloat. The great tubular bridges and the *Great Eastern* steamship sprang from the same origins and even the same site.

Ten

Fairbairn's Resignation: the Great Dispute

Barely a fortnight after the first tube of the Conwy bridge entered service, Fairbairn wrote to Stephenson suggesting that the time had come for him to resign. It can hardly have been a surprise for the relationship had become increasingly strained and there had been rumblings from Fairbairn about resignation the previous May. What part Clark had played in fomenting the disagreement is open to speculation but, from his point of view, Fairbairn's departure would lead to his own position being greatly enhanced and with no one to answer to but Stephenson. Clark had risen a long way in two years and his hand was strengthened with his brother as a personal assistant.

In fairness, it should be said that it may, in any case, have suited Fairbairn's book to resign at this stage, for his salary was a pittance compared with what he could earn as the master of an engineering works, employing as many as 2,000 men. Moreover, the Millwall shipyard had long been unprofitable and a constant drain on the Manchester enterprise. Fairbairn had built several small canal steamers at Manchester after 1830, and seeing the opportunities opened his Millwall yard on the Thames in 1835. With his reputation, work was plentiful despite fierce competition but, although the yard constructed about 100 vessels annually, there were continuous and mounting losses. These culminated in a sale of the yard finalised in 1848 and during this critical period there was much that needed attention at home in preference to pulling chestnuts out of the fire for an ungrateful Stephenson.

Fairbairn's letter of resignation, written at Manchester on 16 May, had probably not been received by Stephenson when he spoke at a celebratory dinner given at Conwy the following day, but Fairbairn took such offence at certain aspects of the speech, which was widely reported, that he immediately confirmed his resignation in a further letter on 19 May. When, by 22 May, neither letter had been acknowledged, Fairbairn wrote a formal letter of resignation to the directors. To Fairbairn's discomfiture, on receipt of this letter the directors reneged on their original terms on which they had made the appointment and required the resignation to be submitted through Stephenson. It was all done in a civilised manner, but there is little doubt of the pent-up emotions underlying the restrained language. Fairbairn was a proud man and felt his reputation had been publicly slighted. It was obvious from the tenor of Stephenson's speech that he, with a nod towards his 'closet companion' Clark, was reserving for himself any fame and credit was going.

What particularly aroused Fairbairn's ire was a repetition of the specious claims regarding a bridge at Ware and priority for the original concept of cellular construction. This apocryphal structure was never built, and when pressed on the matter by Fairbairn, Stephenson had produced a drawing of a primitive plate girder supplied by Fox, Henderson & Co. for the Northerb & Eastern Railway. Previously Stephenson had claimed that the bridge was to carry the Cambridge Road over the Lea Navigation. In fact, a bridge of a different design was built at this point, which local folk memory attributes to George Stephenson. Furthermore, Fairbairn and Hodgkinson were given little credit for the vital part they had played in developing an ill-formed concept into an accomplished reality. Clark on the other hand, was rewarded with a fulsome tribute, but the audience was left in no doubt as to who deserved the lion's share of the credit – Stephenson himself.

Fairbairn's immediate response was to pick up his pen and write a book setting forth the story of the tubular bridges and his part in their creation. Publication caused a considerable furore both within the engineering profession and among a wider public, especially in light of the high reputation Fairbairn enjoyed among the scientific community. There were those who thought that Fairbairn deserved equal credit with Stephenson, but there were others who felt that such a public disagreement was unseemly and did Fairbairn's cause no favours. Comments in the *Civil Engineer's and Architect's Journal* were fair but critical:

> *We have not yet the evidence of the whole case before us, and feel it premature to decide upon an ex-parte statement. We, moreover, are anxious to avoid participating in a contest in which too much of the gall and bitterness of jealousy had been exhibited. But we have enough evidence at least to be quite certain that the discussion has throughout been too strongly marked by the absence of mutual concessions and has been caused solely and entirely by feelings of distrust and a jealous concealment or reserve, which seem absolutely incompatible with a pure love of science.*

A paper war developed between the soldier and journalist, Sir Francis Bond Head, and Thomas Fairbairn, replying on his father's behalf. Head, among other things a director of the LNWR, awarded undivided credit to Stephenson, and quoted very selectively from the evidence the latter gave to the parliamentary committee in 1845. Thomas retaliated by quoting the evidence unabridged which presented a rather different story. The matter was taken up in correspondence in the railway press and did not simmer down until after August 1850, when at a meeting of the British Association M. Jules Guyot made his claim to the tubular principle to little avail.

Although the bridge was not without its critics, the public perception was that it was the great Stephenson's brainchild, and that he alone deserved the credit. Better informed observers thought that the honours should be shared, but the popular myth, much encouraged by Clark's book, has prevailed over the years and William Fairbairn has, as a result, been denied his proper place in history among the great engineers. In its review of Clark's book, the *Civil Engineer's and Architect's Journal* took the view that Fairbairn was only a paid assistant and acting under Stephenson's orders.

The Builder, a more down-to-earth publication, took a different stance, quoting extensively from Fairbairn's book but remaining firmly on the fence, leaving any judgement in the hands of its readers. While publication of the book could not be ignored, the editor could see little profit in taking sides.

The *Mechanic's Magazine* tells of an article in *The North British Review* attributed to Sir David Brewster, an eminent scientist and one of the earliest members of the Institution of Civil Engineers, giving as usual sole credit to Stephenson. This eminent author later confessed to being misled by a pamphlet published by Latimer Clark, nowhere in which does Fairbairn's name appear and after studying the history of the bridges he unequivocally awarded the major credit to Fairbairn. The editor commented:

> To talk, after this, of Mr Fairbairn's being entitled only to a secondary and subordinate place in the affair, is to outrage all truth and propriety. We can regard with profound pity the hallucination which has betrayed a man of Mr Stephenson's genius and worth (this unfortunate episode notwithstanding) into so false a position.

In his Presidential Address to the Institution of Civil Engineers, Sir William Cubitt sought to heal the divisions in the profession. He expressed the opinion that a public conflict between two such eminent members was damaging and that concessions should be made on both sides. Despite this, neither side was prepared to modify their public stance.

An article in the eighth edition of the *Encyclopaedia Britannica*, published in 1856, was contributed by Stephenson, or at least bore his initials, although one of his oldest associates, G.D. Phipps, was believed to have been the true author. It was Phipps who, in the early days of the Forth Street Works, had helped Robert sketch the outlines of *The Rocket* on the floor of the pattern shop. Nowhere is there any mention of Fairbairn's contribution. Failure to offer any recognition eight years after Fairbairn's resignation shows that Stephenson carried this legacy of bitterness to the grave.

Writing after Stephenson's death in his *Industrial Biography*, Samuel Smiles was more forthcoming than before, and stated:

> There is no reason to doubt that by far the largest share of the merit of working out the practical details of those structures and thus realising Robert Stephenson's magnificent idea of the tubular bridge, belongs to Mr Fairbairn.

G. Drysdale Dempsey, who had trained under Stephenson and who wrote much on engineering matters and who also knew Fairbairn personally, was in no doubt, writing:

> That these great works owe their design and construction to those joint labours is clearly evident and, we respectfully submit, amply sufficient to justify the record of the two names of ROBERT STEPHENSON and WILLIAM FAIRBAIRN in an honourable and enduring association.

It was most unfortunate that this bitter controversy arose, but work on the bridges was sufficiently far advanced for all major decisions to have been made. Clark, assisted by his brother, was awarded overall supervision of the ironwork and elevated to the rank of resident engineer, while Ross and Forster, the more experienced engineers, and their assistants were fully capable of maintaining general site control, while Moorsom was always on hand to deal with labour problems. The critical time would arise when the first tube at Menai was ready for floating out, which would not be until June the following year, 1849.

It would be idle to suggest that either Fairbairn or Stephenson were entirely in the right. For a start, they were two proud men and, moreover, Fairbairn was fourteen years the senior and not accustomed to accepting a subordinate role. He knew too that in the beginning Stephenson had been entirely dependent on him, while he could get along very well on his own, and was concerned that, while the Conwy bridge was going up, his own business was languishing and financial storm clouds were on the horizon. He was at one time perilously near bankruptcy. He had played fair by Stephenson and seen the matter through to a point where the project would proceed under its own momentum and there was little left for him to do.

Stephenson, for all his virtues, was not always an easy man to get along with. Temperamentally he was very different to Fairbairn, subject to fits of depression and indecision, prey to black tempers when crossed and in indifferent health. Stephenson's claim in his Conwy speech to have invented the concept of cellular construction proved to be the proverbial last straw for Fairbairn though he had seen fit to ignore it when it was first mentioned in a private letter some time before.

Such claims and counterclaims for priority in inventions have always bedevilled the history of technology and frequently provided rich pickings for the legal profession rather than the unfortunate inventors. In this case, it was Fairbairn's pride rather than his pocket that was hurt. Perhaps George Parker Bidder, speaking in another context, was right when he said that more credit is due to a man who takes an unformed idea and carries it through to perfection than to the man who has the idea but does nothing with it.

Stephenson could be magnanimous when not crossed, and the following extract from a speech made at Newcastle after the completion of the High Level Bridge shows a more generous spirit than that of his father in awarding credit:

If you would read the biographies of all your old distinguished engineers, you would be struck with the excessive detail into which they were drawn; when intelligence was not so widely diffused as at present, an engineer like Smeaton or Brindley had not only to conceive the design but had to invent the machine and carry out every detail of the conception; but since then a change has taken place and no change is more complete. The principal engineer now has only to say 'let this be done' and it is speedily accomplished, such is the immense capital and such the resources of the mind which are immediately brought into play. I have myself, within the last ten or twelve years, done little more than exercise a general superintendence and there are many other persons here to whom the works referred to by the chairman [this reference is to the Britannia, High Level and Royal Border Bridges] *ought to be almost entirely attributed. I have had little or nothing to do with them beyond giving my name and exercising a gentle control in some of the principal works.*

There seems to have been an inborn trait in the Stephenson character which led to claims for credit to which they were not strictly entitled, and George Stephenson was as guilty of this as any. Yet much blame must be laid at the door of many biographers whose true field was closer to hagiography if not fiction. George considered himself rightly entitled to credit for his son's achievements on the ground that it was he who had fathered the boy and attended to his education and upbringing, and a father's pride is not altogether discreditable.

Fairbairn's dispute with Robert Stephenson was of a different nature, for the latter found himself on a public pedestal which he shared only with Brunel. Joseph Locke was a great engineer, but there were many others, too many to name and they did not receive the same degree of public recognition. Any suggestion by Fairbairn that he too should share the limelight was anathema to Stephenson. To persuade Fairbairn to deputise for him on the construction of the tubular bridges he had been forced to concede joint responsibility in all things, but to accept publicly what was implicit in the company minutes was intolerable.

It is most unlikely that Fairbairn would have bridged the Menai Strait, or would even have developed the box girder, had his attention not been drawn to the problem and his advice sought. He had an ailing shipyard and too many other irons in the fire. It is equally unlikely that Stephenson would have bridged the Menai Strait relying on his own resources. He had struggled long enough before meeting Fairbairn and had found no solution. A more generous public acceptance by Stephenson of Fairbairn as a partner in the enterprise would have cost him nothing but it went too much against the grain. In years to come George Robert Stephenson's successful attempt to destroy the character and reputation of a sick and dying Alexander Ross displays the Stephenson envy of other successful engineers at its most despicable and deserves no further comment.

Eleven

William Fairbairn's Box Girders

The primary aim of Fairbairn's experiments at Millwall was to establish the practicability of Stephenson's concept of a tubular girder large enough to allow the passage of a train, and to decide the most favourable shape for the tube.

At quite an early stage, Fairbairn visualised the principle as being applicable to small to medium spans where the box formation was advantageous over single web girders which, as then designed, possessed poor lateral and torsional resistance. Hitherto, apart from the clumsy trussed cast-iron girder first introduced for railway use around 1832, railway engineers had been obliged to rely on cast-iron or masonry arches for all but the shortest spans. Arches were frequently impracticable where riverbanks were low, since the traditional humpback bridge was obviously ruled out and expensive approach embankments were unavoidable. The bowstring or tied arch overcame this problem but was heavy and expensive. The box girder, on the other hand, offered the benefits of a flat soffit, much larger spans and superior stiffness.

Fairbairn possessed a well-developed entrepreneurial instinct, and seeing glowing future prospects he suggested to Stephenson that they should jointly take out a patent for box girders. This suggestion was not well received by Stephenson, who had a principled objection to patents on the ground that they inhibited development. Perhaps he had in mind James Watt's frustration when he found that Pickard had patented the crank, or Watt's subsequent attempts to create a monopoly by use of his own steam engine patents. Undeterred, Fairbairn took out Patent 11,401 dated 8 October 1846 for 'Improvements in the construction of iron beams for the erection of bridges and other structures'. He later wrote:

> *The patent for wrought-iron girder bridges was a joint affair between Mr R. Stephenson and myself. It was in my name as the inventor but he paid half the expense, and was entitled to one half the profits, but it ultimately became a dead letter and was abandoned by Mr Stephenson.*

Fairbairn subsequently built over 100 box girder bridges including swing and lifting spans. Stephenson was responsible for only four, similar in principle but differing substantially in design and these will be described separately.

The year 1846 was marked by several developments in machinery for the working of iron. In April, Charles May of Ipswich patented an hydraulically operated machine for punching, riveting and shearing metal plates and sections, which greatly improved productivity. At the end of 1845 James Garforth of Dukinfield had developed an improved form of steam riveting machine and in July 1846 W.V. Wennington introduced a machine for cutting plate and sheet iron which avoided the distortions caused by earlier methods. As early as 1844 Kennedy & Vernon of Liverpool had started rolling H and Z sections. The stage was set for developing more sophisticated iron structures.

It was once again Charles Vignoles, never afraid to innovate, who first commissioned a bridge of the new design to cross the Leeds & Liverpool canal on the Blackburn & Bolton Railway, together with a second similar bridge over a road. These were double-track three-girder bridges with spans of 60ft, designed and tested to carry 1 ton per foot run. Unusually, tests were made for the effects of impact loads by running locomotives over wedges up to $1\frac{1}{2}$in high placed on the rails and measuring the extra deflection. The bridges passed with flying colours, and it would seem that no further attention was given to the effects of impact until the Royal Commission of 1847. It was estimated that at a cost of £900, each the bridges were over £500 cheaper than a trussed cast-iron girder type. There followed two similar bridges commissioned by James Thomson for the Liverpool & Bury Railway. Thomson is worthy of remembrance as having engineered the first two wrought-iron lattice girder bridges to be built in England, at Darcy Lever and Burnden, near Bolton, where some of the original 1848 trusses may still be seen as parapet girders.

The idea quickly become popular, though not with Stephenson who rejected Fairbairn's offer in January 1846 of box girders for crossing the Dee at Chester, although John F. Bateman, Fairbairn's son-in-law, had prepared detailed drawings. What resulted is history. Two spans of 150ft were built for the floating landing stage at Liverpool and there was also a vertical lifting span built across a road on the approach to the North Dock. This could be raised to allow high vehicles to pass beneath, but permitted the passage of ordinary traffic. As time went on Fairbairn developed his designs. At Perth in Scotland, a swing bridge carried the Dundee & Perth Railway over the River Tay. In Ireland there were two swing bridges on the Midland & Great Western Railway. One at Galway over Lough Atalia, a sea lough, had a swing span of 157ft and there was a smaller one over the River Tuir at Ballinasloe. The Galway bridge is reputed never to have opened again after the official inspection in 1851 despite local interests having campaigned vigorously for its provision. Such were the powers of navigational interests in those days. The rotating mechanism has been removed in recent years. A three-span fixed girder bridge, the Cahir Viaduct, still carries the Waterford & Limerick railway over the River Suir, where the centre span is 150ft. From its configuration it may have designed originally as a continuous beam for the engineer William Le Fanu. Unusually this bridge has only a single top cell and possibly this was ordered by the engineer to make maintenance easier. This viaduct, although reduced to a single line, is still in service and it is probably the last of Fairbairn's bridges to remain virtually unaltered. In addition, on the same line there was a box girder bridge of 48ft span of similar age over the Tipperary road.

The most enthusiastic user of box girder bridges was John Fowler, whose name is more commonly linked to his greatest work, the Forth Bridge, where he shared the credit with Benjamin Baker. As engineer of the Manchester, Sheffield & Lincolnshire Railway east of Sheffield, much of which runs through country with low river banks, he commissioned a number of box girder bridges. At Gainsborough, where the Trent is some 300ft wide, he had originally planned a three span trussed cast-iron girder bridge comparable to that which failed at Chester. Fortunately, the disaster at Chester came in time to save

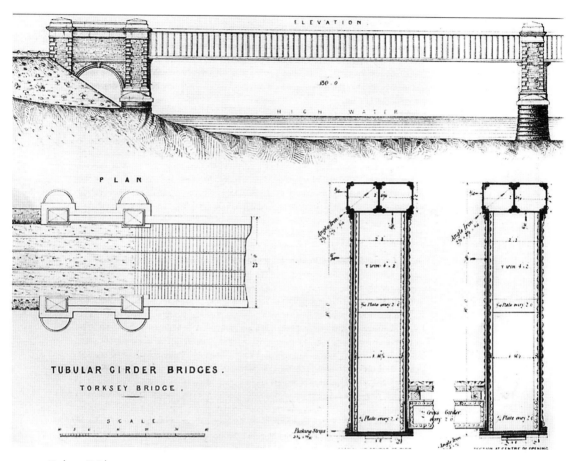

ELEVATION.

150·0'

HIGH WATER

PLAN

TUBULAR GIRDER BRIDGES.

TORKSEY BRIDGE.

SCALE

Torksey Bridge.

him from his folly and a Fairbairn bridge having two 150ft spans was chosen instead. This has been replaced in recent years. A few miles upstream at Torksey, Fowler designed and Fairbairn built a similar bridge with two 130ft spans. Both these bridges were built by assembling the girders in one length on the approach embankment and rolling them out over the river, thus avoiding obstruction to a heavily used tidal waterway. While the Gainsborough bridge had been approved by Capt. Wynne RE in 1848, at Torksey Fowler came up against the redoubtable Capt. Simmons RE, who had demolished Stephenson's defence at Chester. This was to become a *cause célèbre*, and the arguments occupied four consecutive meetings of the Institution of Civil Engineers.

Fairbairn opened the first meeting with a paper on tubular bridges. This was received with something less than due respect by some of the young lions present. Fairbairn was annoyed, particularly as Fowler had ventured to modify his standard design, and he is said to have taken offence and walked out. The point at issue, according to Simmons, was that stresses in part of the girders exceeded 5 tons per square inch. This figure had no statutory force and Fowler, like most of his colleagues, did not feel himself bound by it. One outcome of the Chester failure had been that full responsibility for the safety of bridges was deemed to fall on the owning company and its engineer. The Inspector's position was only advisory since, for a start, he could not be held responsible for hidden defects, a common enough problem with cast-iron girders. The professional engineers, Brunel prominent among them, were fighting their corner, lest as they feared progress and innovation should be stifled by pettifogging civil servants from the Railway Commissioners.

In defence of his bridge, Fowler argued that the two spans constituted a continuous beam and cited experiments carried out by I.K. Brunel and C.H. Wild, while William Pole produced an elegant mathematical analysis to show that the bridge was fifty per cent stronger than Simmons was giving it credit for. Simmons remained unconvinced, although at around the same time he was prepared to take Stephenson's word for it when somewhat similar claims were made for the Britannia Bridge. As the weeks passed by the GNR, which was desperate to use the Torksey Bridge as part of its main line, pending the opening of the direct line over the Newark Dyke Bridge, started to use its political and commercial muscle in Parliament and Whitehall. Simmons had stood his ground manfully against the cohorts of the Institution, but the Railway Commissioners eventually bowed to pressure and gave permission for the bridge to open at the company's risk. Though long disused, the Torksey Bridge is listed Grade II★ and there is every prospect of its renovation by Sustrans for a cycleway.

Among the few box girder bridges built by Fowler in Lincolnshire still remaining in use is the Stamp End Bridge on the Market Rasen line on the southern outskirts of Lincoln. Although nothing remarkable in size, it was opened in 1848 and after being twice strengthened, it still carries heavy oil trains. Even after the expiry of the patent in 1860, Fowler himself had earlier supplied them to Australia and Canada. They appear never to have caught on in India, a major export market for large bridges, since a proposed box girder bridge over the Indus at Attock was never built. One argument advanced in its favour was that the high sides would protect trains from sniper fire.

Two bridges were supplied to the Inverness & Aberdeen Junction Railway. There was a single-track bridge over the Findhorn, with three spans of 150ft built in 1885, which continues to give good service. The larger double-track bridge crossed the Spey, with a single span of 230ft. This gave rise to an extensive correspondence in 1858 between Capt. Tyler RE (a writer of voluminous letters to his employers), Fairbairn and Joseph Mitchell (the company's engineer who was much-respected in the Highlands). Tyler too had been reading Edwin Clark's book and had complained that when fully loaded the maximum stress would exceed the 5 tons per square inch which by then had become the norm. Nonetheless, he was prepared to pass the bridge if only a single track was laid. The whole line at that time was single, but a double line bridge had been ordered from Fairbairn with future doubling in view. Fairbairn insisted that he had been at the game for many years and that in his opinion the structure was adequate for double-track use. The situation reached a deadlock, with neither Fairbairn nor Tyler prepared to give ground, but finally, losing all patience, Mitchell pointed out to Fairbairn that he had contracted to build a bridge to meet Board of Trade requirements and it was up to him to strengthen the bridge where necessary. This he reluctantly did. The problem lay with Fairbairn's empirical formula of 1846 which failed to take sufficient account of the effects of increased stresses in longer spans. All Fairbairn's 1846 and subsequent designs were based

Capt. Sir Henry Whatley Tyler RE (1827-1908), Inspector of Railways in 1853, Chief Inspector from 1871 to 1877, Chairman of the Westinghouse Brake Co. (England), Member of Parliament between 1880 and 1892. He was also the son-in-law of Pasley.

on breaking loads established experimentally at a time when the concept of stress was unknown.

The last major use of Fairbairn's box girders was to replace decayed timber arches on the Dinting Vale and Etherow viaducts on the Manchester to Sheffield line via Woodhead. When Joseph Locke had taken over construction of the line from Vignoles he had specified timber arches for reasons of economy. Locke did not like iron, as he told the 1847 Royal Commission later. Erection was under the supervision of Alfred Janistreet Jee, a promising young engineer who supervised the boring of the first Woodhead Tunnel, but he later died when working in Spain when a locomotive turned over on some newly laid track. Dinting had five arches of 125ft span and Etherow two of 125ft and one of 150ft. By 1854 timber decay had rendered them precarious and, although Jee attempted to add iron bracing, by 1858 passengers were refusing to travel over it so he recommended the use of large box girders made continuous, with track on top. It was a requirement of this contract that single line traffic should be maintained at all times since some seven trains a day crossed the viaducts, latterly in imminent danger.

The delicate operation was carried out successfully with no serious accidents or stoppage of traffic. The new girders were assembled on the approaches and rolled out over the timber structure, which was then dismantled. It was supervised by Fairbairn himself and the company's new engineer, Charles Sacré. The whole operation on both viaducts was carried out for what now seems the modest sum of £28,700. By 1919 the increasing weight of traffic called for strengthening. This was achieved with little regard for appearance by building new brick piers between the original stone structures. Today both viaducts remain in use, although with the closure of the Woodhead tunnel they carry a

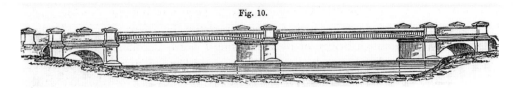

Fig. 10.

Gainsborough bridge.

fraction of their former traffic. However, proposals to reopen the Woodhead route may mean that they will once again come into their own.

Little is known of the Canadian bridges supplied by Fairbairn except for one on the Great Western Railway of Canada where, in 1860, a box girder bridge was erected over the Desjardins Canal to replace a timber bridge which had failed disastrously in 1858. This was a swing bridge offering a clear channel of 66ft when open, and of standard type with the track passing between the girders which were 9ft deep over the turntable tapering to $3\frac{1}{2}$ft at the extremities. Possibly Fairbairn had profited from his dispute with Capt. Tyler over the Spey Bridge, for the report in *The Engineer* makes a point that the maximum stress would never exceed $3\frac{1}{2}$ tons per square inch, or one sixth of the breaking load. There is some evidence that Fairbairn had supplied bridges to India around the same period, since Lambert, his foreman in charge of the erection, had only just returned from similar work there. Unfortunately nothing is known of them except that they were not of the box type. Certainly in Australia Fairbairn supplied a lattice girder bridge in 1860 to cross the Yarra at Cremorne in Victoria but again no details are known.

Back in Canada in 1866 a bridge having three 100ft spans was erected across the St John River in New Brunswick at a point called Hammond River. From the description and drawing, this was copy of a Fairbairn box girder, including two top cells. The patent had expired in 1860 so the engineer, Mr A.L. Light MICE was, like John Fowler in Australia, free to copy the design for his own purposes.

In Australia Fairbairn supplied and erected the Barwon Iron Bridge at Geelong in the State of Victoria. A small erection team of eight skilled men, headed by Foreman Croll was sent out from England in 1855, but delays in constructing the foundations meant that completion was not until 1859. With a span of nearly 210ft it remained for twenty-one years the longest span in Australia. John Fowler was responsible for several Australian bridges, three of which so closely resembled Fairbairn's original concept that, in appearance at least, they could easily be mistaken for the master's work. The main difference between their design philosophies was that Fowler deducted the area of rivet holes when calculating the effective area of the tension flange. Fairbairn's own experiments on riveted joints had convinced him that this was not necessary. The effect of Fowler's design was that nearly equal sections were used top and bottom which Fairbairn considered to be wasteful of metal, merely adding dead weight.

The three Fowler box girder bridges were firstly at Penrith in New South Wales where the Victoria Bridge of 1863 had three spans of 185ft; next the Menangle Bridge of 1864 across the Nepean river with three spans of 160ft each; and lastly the Keilor Bridge of 1868 in Victoria over the Maribyrnong, a road bridge with a single span of 135ft. All three were fabricated at the Canada Works, Birkenhead, and shipped out, but half the Menangle Bridge was lost in a shipwreck which delayed completion by a year. All three bridges resemble the Gainsborough Bridge of 1849 in having a largely decorative arch rib across the web. Menangle suffered a similar fate to Etherow and Dinting by being strengthened in 1907 by the introduction of intermediate brick piers. Variations on the box girder theme were used elsewhere in Australia, the largest being at Tarradale in Victoria, built in 1862 with five deck spans of 130ft made continuous. This too suffered the indignity of having intermediate steel trestles added in 1933 but its Fairbairn ancestry is clearly visible.

Stephenson's Box Girders

Stephenson was not blind to the benefits of the box girder principle, and on his instructions four were built. In broad principle, they resemble Fairbairn's patent, but Stephenson chose to make the top chords of cast iron on grounds of economy and simplicity of construction.

The first was designed and erected by R.B. Dockray at Camden Station on the London & Birmingham Railway. Dockray was resident engineer on the southern section and a respected member of the Stephenson team, and responsible for extensive developments at the Camden Station. The span was 60ft and it carried a roadway 28ft wide over four lines. The top consisted of cast-iron I-sections, lying flat, and bolted together end to end. The sides were 9ft high overall of light boilerplate bolted to the top castings and to vertical castings within the tube at every joint about 4ft apart and angle iron stiffeners were riveted in between. The internal cavity was 1ft 5in wide. The bottom flange was attached to the sides by angle iron and rivets, and cast iron cross girders 4ft apart rested on this. The road deck was supported on corrugated iron sheeting. The general impression is of a very lightweight structure and its eventual fate is unknown.

The three more important underbridges were in the Newcastle area, two at Gateshead on the approaches to the High Level Bridge, while the third (of which little is known) crossed the Great North Road near Alnwick. The bridge at Half Moon Lane, Gateshead, was something of an afterthought being forced on the company by collusion between the Town Council and the Railway Commissioners to force the removal of an existing level crossing. It crossed a triangular junction of roads and was only 35ft on the short side while extending to 75ft span on the longer side. The generous 30ft wide deck was divided by a central girder of 55ft span. The design of the box girders was broadly similar to those at Camden but of much heavier construction and tapered slightly from 18in at the bottom to about 14in at the top flange. The depth of the girders was 7ft. The most important difference as that the cross girders at 9ft centres were suspended by $2\frac{1}{2}$in bolts from the cast-iron tops. This parallels Fairbairn's first bridges for Vignole, but the suspension of cross girders while relieving the tubes of torsion was soon rejected as potentially dangerous.

The larger of the bridges at Gateshead was a skew span of 98ft at West Street, again with three girders 9ft 3in in depth and either 16in or 18in wide at the top. The tops of both bridges, like that at Camden, were finished with decorative castings.

Stephenson displayed no further interest in small box girders and no more were built of the types discussed here.

Twelve
Stephenson's Egyptian Bridges

Apart from the later Victoria Bridge in Canada the only other tubular bridges built on Stephenson's orders were three on the Alexandria & Cairo Railway and these were not of the through type but plain box girders with the track carried on top. The route had been surveyed in 1850-1851 by Henry Swinburne who later became section engineer on the southern section under M.A. Borthwick, the resident engineer. A trusted assistant, Swinburne had travelled out to Egypt with Stephenson on his yacht and had carried out his survey while 'The Chief' was cruising on the Nile, recuperating from years of overwork. At home, the Brotherton Bridge affair was quietly simmering and awaiting Stephenson's return. A contract was signed between Abbas Pacha and Stephenson on 12 July 1851 and work on site commenced the following year.

In traversing the Nile Delta three major navigable waterways had to be crossed – the Rosetta and Damietta branches of the Nile and the Karrineen Canal. Initially, bridging the Rosetta branch was deemed impracticable for lack of firm foundation conditions and steam ferries were planned but work went ahead on the Damietta branch near Benha and the Karrineen Canal at Birket el Saba. At Benha, there were eight box girder spans of 80ft and 6ft 6in depth, with a central swing span of 154ft, providing two clear channels of 60ft each when open. Wrought iron tubular piers of 7ft diameter were sunk 35ft below the lowest water level. The bridge over the canal at Birket el Saba was similar in construction but smaller, with two spans of 70ft and two channels of 43ft each when the swing span was open. The design was attributed to George Robert Stephenson and his assistant, George Barling, but Benjamin Prior Stockman, another assistant, was responsible for the design of the ironwork. The contractor for the line as a whole was Edward Price of London and all the ironwork for the first two bridges was supplied by Grissell & Co., also of London, one of the largest building contractors in Britain. Both bridges were started in May 1853 and completed by October 1855. Some 10,000 pressed labourers were employed on the railway, working under an armed military guard to prevent desertion. Robert Stephenson expressed concern at the treatment meted out to what was virtually slave labour, but there was little he could do as they were Government employees. Even when the line was open, the labourers and their families were forced to trudge from site to site along the line in the searing heat of the Egyptian sun.

The design of the ferries over the Rosetta branch was simple, consisting of little more than a platform to accommodate the wagons, supported on a flat bottomed pontoon and hauled by chains driven by a steam engine. The platforms could be raised or lowered to suit varying water levels by manually operated winches (for labour and indeed life was cheap in Egypt). The design of the engines was attributed by Robert Stephenson to Charles Heard Wild, the promising young engineer who had worked with Edwin Clark on the Welsh tubular bridges. Wild had moved on to join Fox, Henderson & Co. on the

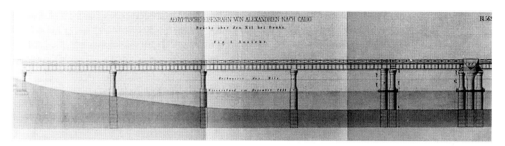

Nile bridge at Benha.

design and erection in Hyde Park of the Crystal Palace for the Great Exhibition of 1851. When the exhibition closed the structure was sold to the Crystal Palace Co., and Wild became resident engineer when the building was dismantled and re-erected and extended on a new site at Sydenham Hill in South London. The work was completed satisfactorily with much credit to Wild but he was instructed to design and build two towers intended to hide the flue pipes from the heating furnaces (there had been no heating at Hyde Park) and to carry large water tanks to supply the fountains in the grounds, designed by Sir Joseph Paxton.

It must have been around this time that Wild showed unmistakable symptoms of the brain disorder which would lead to his death in a few years. The design of his towers was criticised by Brunel, a director of the company, and Paxton then decided that the water tanks should hold 1,500 tons instead of the 500 tons originally specified. Wild's towers were almost completed but he was unceremoniously edged out by Brunel, and was reported to have gone abroad for his health. He next turned up in Egypt, working for Stephenson but not listed as part of the official engineering establishment. Stephenson could be generous to those who had served him well but who had fallen on hard times and did his best for Wild, but when the latter returned to England after a couple of years he was no better. Within three years he had died in a hospice for the terminally insane, almost certainly from tertiary syphilis, then incurable and the bane of all ranks of society, though the quack doctors prospered greatly from it. Indeed in years to come it was to destroy a future Prime Minister.

Possibly, in the light of experience gained at Benha and the inconvenience of the ferries, it was decided in 1857 to construct a similar but larger bridge at Kaffre Azzayat on the Rosetta branch, the railway by that time having reached Suez. On this occasion the piers were of 10ft diameter and sunk 60ft below the bed of the river using Hughes' compressed air process. The design was again claimed by G.R. Stephenson, assisted as before by B.P. Stockman. There were nine spans of 114ft and the swing span over 200ft in length, provided two 80ft channels. The bridge took only seventeen months to build and was completed a few months before Robert Stephenson's death. The resident engineer was a Mr McLaren, possibly the same John McLaren who supervised the ironwork at Britannia and Conwy. The contractor was again Edward Price of London and, on this occasion, all ironwork was shipped out from the Canada Works at Birkenhead. The bridge was opened on 25 May 1859.

Thirteen

The Victoria Bridge, Montréal

The tubular bridges at Conwy and Britannia were a desperate remedy for a desperate situation. Structurally they were to prove a blind alley in bridge development. It was not that they failed in their purpose for they performed their duties admirably and continued to do so under conditions that Stephenson and Fairbairn could never have imagined in 1845. Cost-wise, though, they were a strain on a well-founded company with good prospects of future traffic receipts. The fourth and largest of the train-sized tubular bridges was to prove a great and continuing financial burden on its builders, the Grand Trunk Railway of Canada, a somewhat speculative venture whose traffic revenues never reached the levels that its promoters had anticipated.

In the early 1850s the Canadian economy depended mainly on transport by water up the St Lawrence to Lake Ontario, which was linked to the other Great Lakes by the Welland Canal, opened in 1829. However, this could only take ships up to 300 tons. A far greater obstacle was that for six months in the winter ice stopped all navigation and Québec, Montréal and Toronto were effectively isolated. The Canadian Government of the day was anxious to prevent the American railways drawing away this traffic by penetrating Canadian territory from the south at Niagara and Detroit, thus luring away the economic lifeblood of the country to the ports of New York and Boston.

Thomas Brassey, perhaps England's most successful contractor, with a career spanning thirty-seven years and activities worldwide.

The partly completed Victoria Bridge at Montréal in the depths of winter. When the ice broke up in the spring the floes would rise up almost to the tops of the stone piers and exert tremendous force.

In 1852 the Provincial Government invited a consortium of the leading British railway contractors, Peto, Brassey, Betts and Jackson, to undertake a survey of the country with a view to planning a complete railway system for the future. The Member of Parliament for Birkenhead, Sir William Jackson, himself a railway contractor, was placed in charge of the project and Alexander McKenzie Ross, who had so successfully supervised the building of the Conwy Bridge, was invited to become civil engineer. A scheme was planned and submitted for the approval of the 'Railway Bankers' and promoters, Thomas Baring and George Carr Glyn, who were also conveniently the British financial agents for the Canadian Government. Ross was appointed company engineer for the whole project and charged with the design of 'works of art', while the muck shifting and track laying was delegated to four district agents under Betts' control and Ross's overall supervision. Thus, the engineering of the line was left very much in the hands of Peto, Brassey and Betts, a highly regarded consortium with much good work both in the United Kingdom and world-wide to their credit.

Their line was proposed to run from the south bank of the St Lawrence at Québec to a location opposite Montréal and there the river was to be crossed at a point where it widened into a shallow lake with a width of about two miles. Thence, after bridging the St Lawrence, the line was to pass north of the river and Lake Ontario to reach Toronto. An extension west to Sarnia on Lake Huron was to be built by Canadian contractors. In the summer of 1852, Ross made his preliminary survey. He strongly favoured a single-track tubular bridge at Montréal, adopting earlier proposals by Thomas C. Keefer, a

The tubes for the Victoria Bridge under construction showing the travelling gantries like those at Menai.

Canadian engineer whom he consulted, for a rising approach embankment through the shallows on each bank. He managed to convince John Young, another Canadian engineer, who had already been working on plans for a bridge at this point, of the practicability of his scheme. During the spring of 1852, Ross returned to England for discussions with Stephenson and to prepare plans and estimates. Stephenson had virtually retired and was in poor health but, in August 1852, he braved the journey to Canada for the first and last time since he visited Montréal in 1827 on his way back from South America.

Stephenson landed at Portland, Maine, where it was intended that the Grand Trunk would be able to use the ice free port by acquiring the recently built St Lawrence and Atlantic railroad. The whole distance of 292 miles on the uncompleted line from Portland to the south bank of the St Lawrence opposite Montréal was in due course to be rebuilt. Travel over this line was a hair-raising experience for Stephenson. The journey was completed in just under twelve hours at an average speed of 26mph. The virtues of a loco-motive with a leading bogie truck had been appreciated in America since 1828, when Stephenson himself had suggested it to the Baltimore & Ohio Railroad. Nonetheless, they were almost unknown in British practice until 1860, when William Bouch (elder brother of Sir Thomas Bouch) built two for service on the Stainmore line. Until then a rigid wheelbase had still been the norm. The benefits in negotiating the crude flat bottom permanent way, with little and sometimes no ballast, were clearly evident.

On his return to England, Stephenson prepared a generally favourable report, although somewhat optimistic as to the expected traffic and financial returns, and recommended a tubular bridge over the St Lawrence as being the best option. This was despite the fact that, by this date, the economy offered by open web lattice construction was becoming generally recognised, though never by Stephenson himself. Furthermore, to add to the problems arising from the high cost of a tubular bridge, two fateful decisions were made. Under pressure from the harbour interests at Portland the gauge was made 5ft 6in to discourage traffic being drawn off to New York by the American railroads, which even then were predominantly of standard gauge. As A.W. Currie, historian of the Grand Trunk wrote: 'Time proved the broad gauge to be an unmitigated evil, without value in attracting or holding traffic to Portland, Montréal or Québec, or in preventing the rapid expansion of New York.'

Secondly, the permanent way was to be of the British type with bullhead rails in cast-iron chairs, held in place by timber keys. The severe conditions imposed by the Canadian climate led to frequent breakages of the cast-iron chairs made brittle by the extremely low temperatures of the Canadian winter. Even in the summer over-zealous driving home of the keys by the track maintenance crew caused frequent breakages. When Thomas Brassey visited Canada to inspect progress, he saw how European standards of construction were unsuitable for the conditions in Canada and changes were made.

In due course Stephenson was appointed as Consultant for the Victoria Bridge, with Ross as resident engineer. Coincidentally or not, from 1853 until the end of 1857 Samuel Parker Bidder, brother of Stephenson's partner, George Parker Bidder, was appointed general manager. The Grand Trunk was in most respects a contractors' line, since it was they who enjoyed a monopoly for the provision of track and rolling stock as well.

A view of the Victoria Bridge taken the following summer with several tubes completed.

George Harrison, Brassey's brother-in-law, was sent to Canada to report back on suitable locomotive designs. On his return to England he recommended that a factory should be set up in the Liverpool area to manufacture locomotives, as well as iron bridges, rolling stock and permanent way materials with the exception of rails, which were bought in from the rolling mills as were the wrought iron plates and sections. At the instigation of Jackson, a site was found in his Birkenhead constituency. Thus was founded the Canada Works which was to become a major force in railway engineering until its closure in 1889, nineteen years after Brassey's death.

The story of the building of the Canada Works is little known, despite the important part they played in the supply of railway materials over many years. It originally appears in a remarkable company history, *William Heap and his Company*, first published in 1975 by Mr John Millar of Heap & Partners Ltd at Hoylake in the Wirral. Though many changes have taken place over the years, Heap & Partners is a direct descendant of the Canada Works of Peto, Brassey & Betts.

George Harrison was placed in charge of building the new works. On 29 May 1853, he inspected a likely site of nine acres on the banks of the Mersey, which offered the benefits of both rail and deep water access. That afternoon he prepared sketch plans, obtained a budget price from Meakin, a local builder, and took the evening train to London. Next morning he went over the plans with Brassey and with the latter's blessing returned to Liverpool by the afternoon train. The following day, 31 May, Harrison bought the land and placed a verbal order with Meakin. On 4 June the first brick was laid and by October the buildings were completed. These were not temporary structures but built of $13\frac{1}{2}$in brickwork, with boarded and slated roofs and the main workshop alone was 900ft long and 40ft wide.

William Evans, who had been forced into bankruptcy by problems with the foundations of the river pier of the Boyne Viaduct, was placed in charge of the fabrication shop, bringing his Roberts' Jacquard punching machine with him. He was joined by William Heap, whom he had first employed at Conwy as his deputy. Once again the Roberts

Grand Trunk Railway tubular bridge over rapids at St Annes.

Victoria tubular bridge.

machine was to give invaluable service, since every plate for the Victoria Bridge and numerous other large bridges in Canada had to be pre-punched in the Canada Works ready for riveting together on site at Montréal. James Hodges, the engineer in charge of the erection of the bridge, wrote in his book describing its construction:

> *I trust I may be excused for again drawing attention to the extraordinary perfection obtained in the preparation of this ironwork. In the centre tube, consisting of 10,309 pieces, in which were punched nearly half a million holes, not one piece required alteration, neither was there a hole punched wrong!*

It should perhaps be added, with no discredit to the engineers, that this remarkable feat was aided by punching rivet holes undersize and reaming them out when the plates were in position, with a special night shift employed for this purpose.

In 1854 the Canada Works produced its first locomotive, a handsome broad gauge woodburner with a four-wheel leading bogie and a typically generous American cab. This was the first of its type to be built in England and it was followed by others and a similar batch from the Stephenson works at Newcastle. Although the Dundee & Newtyle Railway had operated a locomotive with a trailing bogie as early as 1833, the first British locomotives with leading bogies were introduced by William Bouch of the Stockton & Darlington in 1860, both built by Stephenson. In America the Mohawk & Hudson is generally credited with the first use of a leading bogie in 1832. The idea had in principle been used in the 'Wylam Dilly' of 1812, but to prevent rail breakage rather than as a means of guidance over rough track. It is also reported that the use of a bogie was patented by William Chapman in 1813.

In Canada, Ross was mainly concerned with the construction of the stone piers and abutments of the Montréal Bridge, and in this he was ably assisted by his former colleague, Francis Thompson. After completion of his work for the Chester & Holyhead Railway, Thompson had practised for a while in London, where his second wife died. He married again at the end of June 1853 and within a few days returned to Montréal where, probably on Ross's recommendation, he was appointed architect to the Grand Trunk Railway. Thus he came to play a prominent part in the design of the piers for the Victoria Bridge and for numerous other bridges, together with all stations and other railway buildings. In April 1859, with his work in Canada completed, he returned to London to practise and in 1866 retired to Hastings, where he died in 1895.

Credit for the design of the Victoria Bridge was awarded jointly to Stephenson and Ross, but Stephenson's cousin, George Robert Stephenson (1819-1905), who had gone to work for Robert as an assistant engineer in 1851, was largely responsible for organising the design of the tubes in the office at Great George Street. The detailing he delegated to his chief assistant, Benjamin Prior Stockman. In his application to the Institution of Civil Engineers in January 1880 for full membership, Stockman listed among his qualifications:

> ...in 1852 was engaged by Mr Geo Robt Stephenson, Past-Pres Inst CE as Chief Assistant, which position he occupied for 13 years, and during that time also acted for 7 years in the same capacity to the late Mr Robt Stephenson MP, Past Pres Inst CE, and was entrusted, among other important works, with the details, calculations of strength, estimates and supervision of the construction of the Victoria, St Lawrence Bridge at Montréal, of many tubular and other bridges for East and West Canada and Egypt.

Among his sponsors were several well known names, and he was proposed by George Robert himself, which seems to support the validity of his claims. Stockman consulted closely with Harrison and Evans at the Canada Works and made several inspection visits to Montréal, so he would seem to be entitled to a great deal of the credit for the quality of the ironwork.

The Building of the Victoria Bridge

It was destined to be the last and, in terms of length, by far the greatest of the tubular bridges. In principle, the building of the Victoria Bridge should have presented no major difficulties. In practice, it was a very different story. The greatest depth of water was only 22ft, apart from a narrow central channel, and a rock foundation lay beneath a hard compacted layer of boulder clay, which removed any need for piling. Timber caissons

The jamb [*sic*] of rafts between pier 13 and pier 14.

188ft in length and 90ft in width were filled with stones, floated into position with tugs and sunk to the riverbed, after which the water was pumped out. Before this could be accomplished, the removal of boulders, some weighing as much as $24\frac{1}{2}$ tons, had to be done by blasting underwater, working in a current averaging 7mph. After the completion of a pier, one end of the caisson was removed so that it could be pumped out and floated to its next position.

These less than ideal conditions only applied for a few months in the summer after the spring floods had subsided. For six months of the year the river was frozen and work on the stonework of the piers could only be carried on at the most for four months from August to November. To extend the working season strips of asphalt and felt were used between the stones instead of mortar and once the frosts had ceased the external joints were pointed and grout was run into the inside through vents left in the stonework. After more than eighty years the piers began to show the effects of their annual battering by the ice and in 1942 they were restored by pressure grouting. They still stand today, a tribute to their builders and the design of the sloping icebreaking cutwaters to break up the ice was subsequently widely copied elsewhere.

Outside working conditions were intolerable for several months each winter, and at other times led to strikes by the imported English workers who had never before encountered such cold. Dysentery and cholera outbreaks were rife and delayed the work as well as claiming many lives. Conditions were at their worst during the spring; as the ice started to break up, pieces up to 250ft long were driven by the force of the current against the cutwaters of the piers, and forced up almost to the height of the tubes. Temporary piers and scaffolding on which the tubes were to be assembled were destroyed, delaying work

Caisson for the stone piers.

for weeks until the ice had finally cleared. Even in the summer there were problems from runaway timber rafts and in 1859 disaster threatened when four rafts, driven by a gale, collided with No.14, one of the central piers. Fortunately, serious damage was avoided by breaking up the rafts, an extremely risky operation.

The first cofferdam was towed out on 24 May 1854. The foundation stone of the last pier, the twenty-fourth, was laid on 12 August 1859 and the same day the first revenue-earning train to Portland ran over the bridge. Two months later Robert Stephenson was dead, but he had lived long enough to know that the last and by far the largest tubular bridge, in fact the largest bridge in the world at that date, was completed. An unofficial opening took place amidst great public rejoicing five days later, when more than 1,000 people passed over the bridge. At the peak over 3,000 men had been employed. To signify Royal approval, Her Majesty Queen Victoria graciously permitted the young Prince of Wales to perform the official opening ceremony on 25 August 1860.

The bridge was 6,512ft in length, with twenty-four spans of 242ft and a central navigation span of 330ft. 9,044 tons of iron were used, and received four coats of paint, totalling 128 acres or one fifth of a square mile. At the abutments, the tubes were 36ft above summer highwater level, rising to 60ft at the centre span. The quantity of masonry erected totalled 2,713,095cu.ft, and 2,280,000cu.ft was used in temporary works. Another statistic to note is that the bridge was completed almost eighteen months ahead of schedule and, even more remarkably, for ten per cent under the original estimate. Beyond doubt, Benjamin Chaffey's ingenious materials handling equipment and pumps contributed greatly to this satisfactory outcome.

A suitable source of stone was found sixteen miles west of Montréal, at Isle La Motte on Lake Champlain, and this quarry provided a very hard limestone ideal for construction work. The line of Canada's first railway, the Champlain & St Lawrence, opened in 1836, ran close by. Since the quarry lay on Indian land James Hodges, the resident engineer, had to negotiate with the elders of the tribe. He described how these were not the noble savages of fiction but thirteen miserable dirty-looking old men smoking clay pipes. At first they were disinclined to do business with him because they complained of his extreme youth. Given assurances that Hodges had turned forty years of age they relented and an accommodation was duly reached.

Before leaving England Hodges had commissioned an expensive steam-travelling crane from an eminent firm of engineers to handle the blocks of stone, some of which weighed 10 tons. When erected on site it proved useless, barely able to move itself. Fortunately a Canadian sub-contractor, Benjamin Chaffey, had the wits to devise an overhead crane, carried on timber 'gawntrees' [sic] which covered an area 1,300ft long and 60ft wide, and allowed two men to sort and stack the dressed blocks as they were delivered, 70,000 tons in all. Chaffey was to prove himself to be an exceedingly innovative mechanical engineer and he devised various steam-operated cranes and lifting equipment, which contributed greatly to the early completion. He also devised a steam-operated centrifugal pump for dewatering the caissons which proved greatly superior to the clumsy piston pumps first introduced from England.

In many ways the tubes differed from those designed by Fairbairn for the Welsh bridges, and more closely resembled a conventional plate girder bridge, having no top and bottom cells. Wrought-iron I-section cross girders at about 2ft centres carried the deck and rails while the top flanges of the side girders were extended to form a roof composed of several thicknesses of plates with longitudinal stiffeners, much as Edwin Clark had employed at Brotherton. As in Wales, the sides or webs were made up of vertical plates riveted to tee iron stiffeners at every vertical joint, corresponding with the cross girders which were linked to the sides and floor by triangular gussets. The tubes were 16ft high at the abutments and 22ft high at the centre, and were joined in pairs to limit the expansion movement. The contractor for the erection of the whole of the ironwork was James Hodgkinson.

For the erection of the tubes temporary timber piers were constructed midway between the stone piers, and a pair of timber Howe trusses supported a working platform on which the ironwork as assembled with temporary site bolts. All rivet holes were reamed to size – an arduous job with no form of power tools available – and the following day shift completed the riveting and replacement of the temporary bolts.

Conditions in the $1\frac{1}{4}$-mile long tube were a constant source of complaint by train crews, and after 1872 they were made even worse by the replacement of wood by coal as fuel. In summer with the sun on the tube the atmosphere became almost unendurable during the seven minutes or so taken to pass through even with such protection as was afforded by the large locomotive cabs. Initially, almost as an afterthought, vents were provided in the sides at 60ft intervals but these proved totally ineffective. In desperation a 20in wide slot was cut in the centre of the roof and covered with a monitor and even this drastic action offered only limited relief. What effect it had on the structural integrity of the roof which formed the top chord and main compression member is difficult to tell, but the bridge survived.

Although rumour had it that the rivets on the Britannia Bridge were a constant source of trouble, there is little evidence for this. The Victoria Bridge on the other hand kept a team of riveters fully employed replacing faulty rivets. It was the climate rather than bad workmanship that was to blame. Wrought iron can become brittle at very low temperatures and Hodges reported as much as 73 degrees (F) frost. The effectiveness of riveting depends, as Fairbairn's experiments showed, on the clamping effect caused by the contraction of this rivet on cooling. Further contraction in very cold conditions caused the heads to break off.

In total the bridge had cost £1.5 million, and for many years the interest alone on this was to be a crippling burden on the company. Even so, and including the Victoria bridge itself, the line was capitalised at £11,060 per mile in comparison with £40,000 average for an English line. Much of this saving was due to lower land prices and Government land grants, although land values rose remarkably when the railway surveyors hove in sight. Furthermore, there were no long-drawn-out legal battles before Parliamentary Committees to the benefit only of rapacious lawyers. By comparison, it cost the GNR in England £500,000 just to obtain its Act of Parliament.

By 1897 many of the main lines of the Grand Trunk had been doubled, and the single line bridge was becoming a serious bottleneck. Moreover, brine leaking from refrigerated freight cars had set up severe corrosion. The tubes were replaced by double-track open web girders (of single triangular or Warren type) by widening the tops of the piers, and a road and an inter-urban electric railway were cantilevered out. In the recent years the southern approaches have been greatly changed, but the original piers still remain in use as a memorial to the Victorian pioneers.

During its comparatively short life the Victoria bridge had been criticised not only on account of what was deemed to be its excessive cost but also because of the operating problems previously mentioned. One of its most severe critics was Zerah Colburn, an engineer born in New York in 1833 where he gained railroad and journalistic experience before moving to London to become editor of *The Engineer* in 1858. Six years later he founded his own journal *Engineering* where he preached the superior virtues of everything American. The tubular bridges were a favourite target since Colburn was firmly of the opinion that J.A. Roebling's suspension bridge of 820ft span, completed in 1855 at Niagara Falls, pointed the way forward. He countered the criticism that trains were limited to a walking pace by arguing that a few minutes extra in a journey of many hours was immaterial. Time was to prove Colburn wrong, and when Roebling's bridge was replaced in 1897 it was with a steel lattice structure.

A number of tubular or box girder bridges were built on the Grand Trunk Railway, although by 1897 all had been replaced during doubling of the track. None were attributed to Robert Stephenson and were probably commissioned by A.M. Ross in association with Peto, Brassey & Betts and the Canada Works. In 1857 the English directors instructed Charles Hutton Gregory, a distinguished consultant, to prepare a detailed report on the state of the works in Canada. In August he submitted a generally favourable report and commented on the high quality of the bridges and masonry abutments. He states:

I have rarely seen a work of finer design and execution than the Credit Viaduct, of an extreme height of 121 feet with 8 spans of 96 feet. The wrought-iron girders and tubes are of very good construction... I consider that this line is a Work of which both Engineer and Contractors may justly be proud.

All of the bridges were for a single line, and would appear to have been similar in most respects to the large box girders with the track laid on the top deck used by Stephenson in Egypt on the Alexandria to Cairo line. However, one major bridge having three train-sized tubular girders of 200ft span with thirteen deck-type box girders of 60ft span on the approaches was built in 1856 to cross the Ottawa River at Sainte-Anne-de-Bellevue. This preceded the Victoria Bridge and its existence is not widely known but, in all, only five train-sized tubular bridges were ever built. In only fourteen years the bold concept of 1845 had become outmoded and rejected by a new breed of engineer, backed by a rapid growth in structural theory. The future of long span railway bridges lay with some form of open web or lattice girders.

The building of the Grand Trunk Railway had been an enormous undertaking through country which was largely in its primeval state. Despite all the problems, physical, financial and not least political, that assailed Ross he had battled on at great cost to his health. In the earlier years he had enjoyed the support of Samuel P. Bidder, younger brother of Stephenson's partner, as general manager, but when he returned to England in 1858 an older man took Bidder's place but retired within a couple of years due to ill-health. After completion of the railway, Ross chose to return to England as the years of stress led to a nervous breakdown, which confined him to an asylum. Even then he might have recovered but for a particularly distasteful action by George Robert Stephenson after his cousin's death. Robert was not averse to claiming any credit that was going, but would never have stooped to such chicanery.

When the contract for the Victoria Bridge was signed in 1853, it was stated clearly that Stephenson and Ross were joint engineers for the bridge. At no time did Stephenson play any part in the rest of the railway which was exclusively under Ross's supervision. However, the Stephenson family attempted to claim all the credit for the Victoria Bridge, without any justification and this so preyed on Ross's already disturbed mind that his condition deteriorated, leading to his death at the early age of fifty-seven. An extensive obituary appeared in the *Toronto Leader* on 27 August 1862, but since Ross had never been a Member of the Institution of Civil Engineers no official obituary ever appeared in the country of his birth.

Fortunately for posterity, another engineer, George Tate, who had worked alongside Ross for many years, was so concerned about the lies which were being put about that he wrote an unsolicited eleven-page letter in immaculate copperplate to Ross's brother in London, setting out a full account of their shared experiences. But let the *Leader* have the last word:

In London a scheming unscrupulous clique has, not without success, endeavoured to detract from his worth, a success they owe purely to his mental prostration. In happier times no such effort would have prevailed in England. In Canada, from the first, it has been received only with contempt.

Fourteen

New Developments in Iron Bridges, 1845-1890

The years from 1845 to 1849, during which the tubular bridges were under development, saw a rise in popularity of the trussed cast-iron girder until the collapse of the Dee Bridge in May 1847, and the deliberations of the Royal Commission which followed, led to its rapid demise. Existing bridges were strengthened or propped up and the one at Stockton-on-Tees lasted another fifty years in this condition because it carried only mineral traffic. Where riverbanks were low and a flat soffit was essential, which was particularly true of much of the midland and eastern counties of England, some alternative to the cast-iron girder was essential for all but the smallest spans. Fairbairn's patent box girder of 1846 offered one alternative and its rise and fall has been described in an earlier chapter.

Primitive forms of single web plate girder attempted unsuccessfully to copy Eaton Hodgkinson's cast-iron girder, where the cross-section of the top flange was about one third of that of the bottom flange. The results were disappointing due to failure of the top in compression, but the relative weakness of wrought iron to resist buckling in compression was not then appreciated. Fairbairn's cellular top of 1846 had offered one solution where the limitations of wrought iron in compression were balanced by some 10% extra metal distributed in a form best adapted to increase stiffness. Other bridge designers, in particular Brunel, achieved similar results by using other forms of tubular tops. Having stabilised the tops, weaknesses started to show in the web plates, which in turn buckled under excessive shear stress, though no engineer at that date knew exactly why. The provision of vertical web stiffeners was found to remedy this and by extending these to include the top and bottom flanges the modern single web plate girder evolved. This permitted the use of flat plates in the designs. Perhaps Fairbairn's plate girder, which he designed for the Sheffield Goods Branch in 1855, marked the changeover period. Thereafter there were no fundamental changes until the introduction of steel after its approval by the Board of Trade in 1877 and the use of welding in place of riveting in the 1950s.

In 1850 the long-term future of the iron railway bridge for spans in excess of 80-100ft lay in the triangulated truss, sometimes referred to generally as the lattice girder. The trellis girder was derived from Ithiel Town's timber design, patented in America in 1820 and 1835 and used a complex of flat iron bars crossing at right angles to form the web. Below this span the single web plate girder, which appeared in a multiplicity of forms, would come to dominate the field though smaller trusses were also widely used as for example on Bouch's Penrith to Cockermouth line where there were (and still are) a number of smallish bowstring trusses.

A vast demand for railway bridges in America, many of them of considerable span, produced a flood of new truss designs. Some such as the Pratt were fundamentally sound and have survived until today, as has the English Warren or single triangular girder, widely used in a variety of configurations. The Town, the Long, the Burr, the Howe and other early American designs were best suited for timber construction for which they were originally intended. Timber was available in almost unlimited quantities and large sizes, iron was relatively scarce and expensive and for many years there was a public distrust of iron bridges and not without good reason. Plentiful and cheap though it might be, timber had its faults. Apart from a propensity to rot and to catch fire from passing trains, it was not until recent years with the advent of high duty adhesives that tension joints could be made in timber which did not quickly weaken with use and weathering.

For iron structures, some designs like the Fink & Bollmann trusses were unduly complicated, flimsy in appearance and unstable in practice, as was the Rider truss which became enormously complex with increasing size. By far the most successful design was the bowstring truss patented by Squire Whipple in 1841. His educated approach to bridge design, and the publication of his book on bridges in 1847, is generally considered to mark the beginning of a logical, if not a truly scientific approach to structural design in America.

If early American designers of iron bridges had one thing in common it was a willingness to operate at high levels of stress, leading to fatigue problems that they failed to anticipate. Bridges became weakened over years of use and, coupled with ever-increasing loads, disaster would suddenly strike without warning. If failure ensued, designers were at least willing to learn from their mistakes but this failed to reassure a nervous public, and for many years iron was regarded with distrust as a bridging material. This public resistance coupled with plentiful supplies of timber tended to inhibit iron bridge development in America compared with Britain. A similar situation arose in Britain after the fall of the Tay Bridge in 1879.

The Pratt or N truss, patented in America in 1844, did not appear in Britain until 1865 but the double N truss was used in England in 1859 when the mathematician J.H. Latham

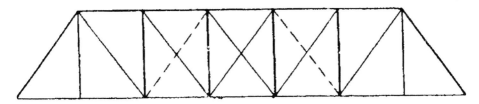

The Pratt or N truss with diagonals in tension. Counter-bracing is common in at least one centre panel.

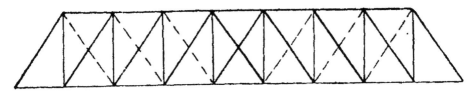

The Howe truss with diagonals in compression and with central counter-bracing.

developed it for a bridge planned for India. In America, it appeared some years later as the Whipple-Murphy or Linville truss. Our home-grown double triangular truss, which should forever be associated with the name of Robert Henry Bow of Edinburgh, was to prove the most popular of all in Britain despite the disadvantage of being indeterminate. Bow devised a graphical method of design, which was favourably received by Clark Maxwell and not long afterwards Allan Duncan Stewart (1831-1894), a mathematician of considerable ability and later chief assistant to Benjamin Baker on the Forth Bridge, worked out a close mathematical approximation.

The American engineer Richard Boyes Osborne (1815-1900), born in London but of Irish parentage, is credited with the first all-iron Howe truss to be built in America, constructed on the Philadelphia & Reading railroad during his return to Europe in 1845 to promote the Howe truss, patented in 1840. Here it was coolly received by Robert Stephenson and at that time any idea which did not pass the Stephenson test did not flourish – whatever its virtues. As Osborne tells in his memoirs: 'Mr Stephenson had evidently 'Tube' on the brain, he would investigate nothing else, and after several days waiting on him he patronisingly gave me a ticket to his tube experiments at Mill Wall [sic] and I removed my despised model.'

A call on Vignoles proved more productive and in due course Osborne found himself resident engineer of the Waterford & Limerick Railway then about to be built. For this line he designed an iron Howe truss bridge of 86ft clear span to cross a road at Ballysimon. So far as can be ascertained, no other Howe trusses were built in the UK for

The first Warren girder bridge on the main line of the GNR at Newark, opened in 1852. It was built to a design by C.H. Wild, adapted by Sir William and Joseph Cubitt, and rebuilt in 1890.

railway work although they proved most popular in America and on the Continent where the timber form continued to predominate. In America the fall of the twelve-year-old iron Howe truss bridge at Ashtabula Creek in 1877, when ninety people died, some in the freezing waters of the creek and others in the fires which raged through the wooden passenger cars, came as a shock to the American public. This was America's equal of the Tay Bridge disaster and initiated wide-ranging inquiries. The failure in tension of an iron casting at Ashtabula led to an extensive review of bridge designs and the use of cast-iron components generally. Even so there continued to be on average twenty-five bridge failures a year in America in the following decade.

The traditional cast-iron arch from the early years of railways was cheap and reliable and continued to remain in favour for many years, but the somewhat clumsy cast-iron tied arch as in the High level Bridge at Newcastle was rapidly replaced by the wrought-iron bowstring girder with diagonal shear bracing. These included Brunel's span of 202ft over the Thames at Windsor, opened in 1849, and the much flatter arches on the Blackwall Extension Railway designed by A.E. Cowper of Fox, Henderson & Co. Unfortunately the shallow spans gave rise to marked vibration problems and within a few years these bridges were replaced, whereas Brunel's larger bridge remains in service, the pride of the Royal Borough of Windsor.

At Chepstow, across the Wye, Brunel had to span 300ft over the deep water channel and to satisfy the Admiralty he was obliged to maintain a clearance of 50ft. He adopted an entirely new principle, which resembled an inverted suspension bridge. The horizontal tube that formed the compression member was slightly cambered by the inward pull from the chains and two massive A frames took the compression load between the tube and the deck. Diagonal chains filled the gaps between the two A frames. It has been suggested that the bridge would have been the earliest example of an inverted N truss had solid members being used in place of chains. In fact, for an unknown number of years prior to its demolition in 1962, the links of the chains had become solid with rust. The Chepstow Bridge opened in 1852 and it is usually regarded as the forerunner of the much larger Royal Albert Bridge at Saltash, with two main spans of 455ft, opened seven years later.

A common feature of both Brunel's bridges was the use of plate girders in the approach viaducts. As might be expected, Brunel would have no truck with Fairbairn's box girders, choosing instead a single web plate girder with a tubular compression member. Nowhere did the spans exceed 100ft. With the great increase in locomotive weights and even after adding additional stiffening to the webs, these approach spans had to be replaced. This was undertaken at Saltash in 1928 but the Chepstow spans survived until a near collapse of one span in 1944 sounded alarm bells. Never perhaps since the failure of the Dee Bridge in 1847 had the factor of safety fallen so close to unity and once again lack of sufficient web stiffeners was to blame. By contrast, Fairbairn's box girders with stiffeners on average every 2ft could not be faulted.

The Hidden Flaw in a Cast-Iron Beam, 1882

While the 1847 Royal Commission sounded the death knell for the trussed cast-iron girder bridge, the simple cast-iron beam was to continue to be used for smaller bridges for many years. No serious failures were reported until an accident at Inverythan on the Great North of Scotland Railway in 1882, resulting from a flawed casting, caused the Board of Trade to issue a recommendation that cast-iron girders should not be used in new work. In practice, though, this in no way amounted to a ban. In 1891 a girder failure on the Brighton main line at Norwood Junction led to a further recommendation that all cast-iron girders should be replaced, but again this was no more than good advice. Since the ultimate responsibility was shared by the companies and their engineers the Board of Trade had no power to enforce this. Numerous sound cast-iron girders remained in service for many years, and some on secondary lines right up until closure. A good cast-iron girder to Hodgkinson's standards was reliable if not overloaded but the hidden flaw was an ever present risk and could remain for years before failing without warning. Existing cast-iron girders reported in use as late as 1895 could deviate greatly from best practice, some being extremely shallow, but as long as the engineers were prepared to certify their safety they remained. New bridges were expensive.

A new generation of formally trained engineers was coming to the fore in the latter part of the 1850s, several having been educated at Trinity College, Dublin, which in 1841 was the first university in Ireland to have a school of engineering. It was in Ireland too that the first iron lattice girders were built, and it was at Queen's College, Galway, that the forces in the diagonals of Warren girders were first evaluated experimentally by W.T. Doyne and Prof. Bindon Blood. The up-and-coming young engineers regarded the tubular bridge as an engineering dinosaur and its protagonists likewise. There was even talk of the old guard cooking the figures in favour of the tubular concept.

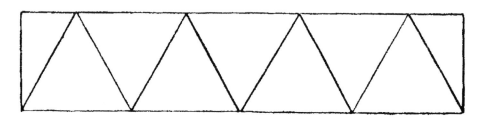

The basic single triangular or Warren truss. The diagonals normally, but not necessarily, form equilateral triangles.

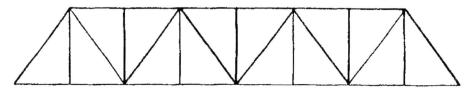

The Warren truss with verticals that are more commonly used today, as in the new Wye Bridge.

The Trussed Wrought-Iron Girder

The success in 1855 of James Barton's open web lattice girder bridge across the Boyne at Drogheda, with a clear span of over 250ft, set the pattern for the years ahead, and the future clearly lay with the triangulated truss.

The simplest of all trusses, the single triangular truss or Warren girder was patented in 1848 by James Warren, an East India merchant, and Willoughby Theobald Monzani, a part time inventor. The Warren girder never attained wide popularity in Britain, though taken up with enthusiasm by James Meadows Rendel and exported to India in large quantities. Its virtue for export lay in its ability to be broken down into convenient sections and erected with the minimum of skilled labour. Warren's patent was taken over and exploited by Edwin Clark and Charles Wild, who claimed a ten per cent royalty for themselves. Stephenson had no time for open web girders and must have been taken aback by these young upstarts, though there seem to have been no hard feelings, and he had mellowed as he relaxed in partial retirement.

In England, the first major Warren type bridge was built across the Newark Dyke on the Great Northern main line, by Joseph Cubitt. It was stated by Cubitt to have been based on a design by Wild (who presumably claimed his commission), and opened in 1852. However, over the years this bridge had increasing problems with wear in its pin joints, particularly where sharp stress reversal took place. As a result it rattled abominably while trains crossed and with ever heavier loadings it had to be replaced in 1890 by a massive Whipple-Murphy bridge designed in house by E. Duncan of the GNR and built by the old established firm of Handyside of Derby. Perhaps the best known of the few Warren truss bridges was the Crymlyn (Crumlin) Viaduct of ten 150ft spans in South Wales, designed and built by T.W. Kennard and opened in 1857. A new patent was awarded to Kennard after certain design modifications which allowed payment of the royalty to be avoided. This was followed by a somewhat similar, smaller viaduct at Meldon in Devon, designed by William Jacomb, opened for a single line in 1874 and doubled five years later.

When the Redcar to Whitby line was started in 1871, the engineer, John Dixon (who later assisted Benjamin Baker with the floating of Cleopatra's Needle from Egypt to London) made use of Warren girders copied from some exported to India. These did not last long, for when the NER later took over the line, their engineer, T.E. Harrison (earlier resident engineer on the Newcastle High Level Bridge), reported scathingly: 'I have never seen work so thoroughly scamped with the viaducts and ordinary bridges so badly designed and as badly executed as to be in a dangerous condition.'

Out went the Warrens and in came single web plate girders, with all the piers being strengthened with additional bracing. At Staithes a wind gauge, now in the National Railway Museum, was fitted and all traffic stopped when winds reached 50mph.

The trellis girder was first developed in Ireland by James Thomson and Sir John Macneill, and was based on the American Town patents. A road bridge of 80ft span was erected over the Dublin & Drogheda Railway and the line itself, opened in 1844, was carried by two similar bridges of 140ft span over the Royal Canal and a Dublin square. Like most prototypes they were not entirely successful and there was much still to be learnt. The main error appeared to be a failure to use proportionately heavier bracing

The former viaduct at Crymlyn in South Wales, showing the Warren trusses as modified by T.W. Kennard. This was the first major use of a tubular trestle-type structure for the piers, which were up to 200ft high. (Photo by Eric de Maré. Crown Copyright. Royal Commission on the Ancient and Historical Monuments of Wales.)

towards the ends of the spans. Thomson went on to engineer the Liverpool & Bury line which opened in 1848. This included two large trellis viaducts at Darcy Lever and Burnden, the first in England. In the early 1880s, they were rebuilt but two of the original main girders in each span were retained as parapet girders and can still be seen. Thomson seduced the wife of Jesse Hartley, the engineer of Liverpool Docks, and they eloped to London just ahead of Hartley wielding a horsewhip. Thereafter he managed the contract by remote control with his brother holding the fort.

The trellis or multi-lattice girder fell out of favour, in all probability because it was expensive to fabricate, having so many components, and being indeterminate its design involved a considerable degree of judicious guesswork leading to extra metal being employed just to be on the safe side! Probably the last major bridge of this type to be built was over the Mersey at Runcorn Gap, opened in February 1869. By that date, its three spans of 300ft each were no longer exceptional. But William Baker, its designer and chief engineer of the LNWR, chose not to follow in the footsteps of Brunel and Stephenson. He was probably unaware of Latham's design a decade earlier and chose a form of truss which had seen twenty-five years' service elsewhere. At 1,700 tons each, the spans are of massive construction and with the easier conditions arising from the introduction of electric traction in 1962 there seems no reason why the bridge should not celebrate its second centenary.

As late as 1881, W.R. Galbraith, consultant to the North British Railway, designed the South Esk Viaduct at Montrose with multi-lattice bracing. This was to replace a ramshackle structure which was the swansong of Sir Thomas Bouch and never carried a passenger train. The choice of bracing was probably to allay public fears of iron bridges generally after the fall of the Tay Bridge in 1879, where the X panels were 27ft wide and criticised for being exceptionally open with little to prevent a derailed train from falling through.

Robert H. Bow and Braced Structures

As early as 1850 an obscure self-styled and largely self-educated civil engineer in Edinburgh, Robert Henry Bow, had published a small treatise on braced structures which appears to have had little immediate impact. Bow's name will be known to many from *Bow's Notation*. In the mid-1850s his fellow citizen, Thomas Bouch, was faced with bridging three deep valleys on the South Durham & Lancashire Union Railway, the famous Stainmore Line. To speed construction Bouch chose iron bridges, and turned to Bow for advice. Bow promoted the X truss, where there are no vertical members except at the ends. Generally the diagonals crossed at right angles though some designers chose a more acute angle to reduce the width of a panel, whereas the larger trusses used vertical members between the Xs for the same purpose, as was done in the Tay Bridge.

The magnificent viaducts at Belah and Deepdale were the result. They bore some resemblance to the Crymlyn Viaduct in having braced tubular trestle piers, but the 60ft clear span trusses were of the X or double triangular type. Belah had a maximum height of 196ft and sixteen spans, while Deepdale was 161ft high with eleven spans. Similar

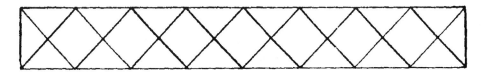

The double triangular or X truss originally promoted by Robert H. Bow.

trusses were used for the seven-span Tees Viaduct which had masonry piers, and where the ironwork was supplied by a familiar name – T.W. Kennard of Crymlyn. The other two were built by Gilkes, Wilson & Co. of Middlesbrough and completed in a remarkably short time since all the parts were prefabricated in their works. Thereafter, Bouch, who shared Robert Stephenson's loyalty to a familiar concept, used the X truss throughout all his future work. It served him well, and many of his X trusses from the first Tay Bridge are still giving good service in Barlow's new bridge of 1884.

The X truss can be described as a double triangular or even a double Warren truss but perhaps deserves to be known as the Bow truss after its original promoter. It seems never to have been patented. In its modified form, the double triangular truss became widely used, and was probably the most popular truss form in the late nineteenth century. This form of bracing is conspicuous in the Forth Rail Bridge, and the Edward VII Bridge at Newcastle of 1906 was probably its last use in a major work.

American truss designs were slow to be accepted in this country. The Pratt or N truss originated in America in 1844 as a timber structure and the first iron versions were exported from the Thames Ironworks & Shipbuilding Co. to Queensland in 1864. It was at this period that as assistant engineer, Callcott Reilly (1829-1900) introduced two N truss bridges on the Horsham & Guildford Direct Line, a single track rural byway despite its name. The larger of the two bridges over the Wey & Arun Junction Canal had a span of 80ft. Reilly rose to become Professor of Civil Engineering at the East Indian Engineering College at Coopers Hill near Windsor. For many years this college had a monopoly of the supply of engineers to the Indian Public Works department, and Reilly's teaching may well have influenced bridge-building technology in India where engineers were more adventurous in outlook than their stay-at-home colleagues and generally more progressive in their thinking.

The GWR was the first to introduce N trusses when replacing a Brunel timber viaduct at St Pinnock, the highest of the timber viaducts at 151ft, which was rebuilt in 1882. Largin Viaduct followed in 1886. After the choice of N trusses for the internal viaduct of the Forth Bridge they rapidly gained popularity especially on the GCR where they were widely used for the strengthening of old box girder bridges as well as for new work on the London Extension and elsewhere.

As mentioned previously, J.H. Latham, Cambridge mathematician and assistant to J.M. Rendel and his son, Alexander Rendel, consultants to the East Indian Railway, designed a bridge for crossing the Jumna utilising double N trusses which consisted in effect of two lines of N bracing spaced half a panel apart. This was a riveted structure and superior to the similar pin-jointed trusses introduced later in America under the name of Whipple-Murphy. Latham failed to secure the fellowship he sought at Clare College Cambridge and became manager of an irrigation scheme in Madras before moving to New Zealand where he took up sheep farming. Sadly, a good bridge designer was lost.

Conservatism generally prevailed in the UK and the riveted double N truss did not appear in use here until introduced by W.H. Barlow, the consulting engineer in the second Tay Bridge of 1887, twenty-nine years after Latham's Jumna bridge. These too became popular as at Newark with the single N truss being restricted to spans of under 250ft.

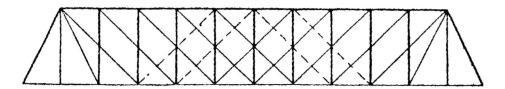

A double N truss originated by Squire Whipple and more generally known as the Whipple Murphy or Linville truss. It was developed in England in 1858 by J.H. Latham.

The first Tay bridge was indeed the longest in the world when built (over tidal waters to be pedantic) but there was nothing innovative in the design, and Thomas Bouch and his designer Allan Duncan Stewart stuck throughout to the well-tried X truss. Nor in fact could they be criticised for this, for no fault was attributed to the truss design and those which escaped the fall were used again and are still in service. On the other hand, Bouch's design for a stiffened suspension bridge to cross the Forth at Queensferry was a strange-looking and ungainly creature, and he reverted to the obsolete trellis construction. William Pole and W.H. Barlow were called upon to report on the design. While raising no objections, they were not prepared to commit themselves to an opinion that it was the best possible – a wise caveat. Even so, with William Arrol as the designated contractor, success might have been achieved. But, on the advice of Astronomer Royal G.B. Airy, the design was based on a maximum average wind force of 10lb per square foot, whereas the Tay Bridge, which had blown down just before the report was published, had been designed for double that wind load.

The really forward-looking development of the late 1880s was Fowler and Bakers' introduction of the balanced cantilever on a massive scale at the Forth Bridge. Even there the simple X bracing predominated rather than the far more complex designs developed in particular in America. There was not the demand in Britain that existed in the United States for spans of great length. By 1876 at Cincinnati, a simple truss span of 515ft had been constructed to be followed by at least twenty-five other truss spans of greater length in the years up to 1910. In 1917, a truss span of 720ft was erected over the Ohio River in Illinois. In India bridges of enormous length were constructed across the wide flood plains of the major rivers but they were remarkable for the number of spans rather than the size.

The years between 1855 and 1895 were more a period of consolidation rather than innovation and it was after this period that an increased understanding of impact forces led to use of the N and double N trusses on a large scale for new works and replacement of older structures. Yet the fifty years from 1840 to 1890 taken overall were the most formative period in British iron bridge development.

Fifteen

The Final Years

By 1970 the Britannia Bridge had seen 120 years of service and according to modern standards was approaching the end of its natural life. No bridge lasts forever, though Benjamin Baker declared that the Forth Bridge would, if kept painted. Now, after many years of neglect, his words have been heeded. Of the other tubular bridges only Conwy remains in service and there the span had been reduced to about 300ft in 1890 to cope with heavier traffic by building additional piers 50ft from each end. The Brotherton Bridge, along with many other inadequate bridges, was replaced around the turn of the twentieth century and the two Canadian bridges were rebuilt a decade earlier when doubling of the Grand Trunk Railway took place.

Not only had the weight of locomotives increased more than fourfold but axle loads had trebled since Stephenson's day. By 1930 bridge engineers had become fully aware of the dynamic forces exerted by locomotives on tracks and bridges, even at low speeds – forces dismissed by Stephenson and many of his contemporaries as negligible or non-existent. The Britannia Bridge continued to soldier on though it must have caused some concern to those responsible for its safety.

Matters came to a head in 1966 when the use of 102 metric ton gross tank wagons, having more than double the capacity of the largest existing tankers, was proposed. The intention was to use them on thirteen main routes, including at a later date that to Holyhead. The Britannia Bridge had needed little major attention apart from painting and lubrication of the expansion rollers since its opening in 1850 and there was concern that the loading conditions over the piers arising from the continuity might have changed with time. The British Railways Research Department at Derby was given the task of assessing the bridge's suitability for the increased loads. The weights imposed on the piers were measured by the use of calibrated hydraulic jacks and the loadings elsewhere measured by the use of mechanical strain gauges.

Clark's declared aim had been to reduce the mid-span bending moments and hence the stresses, by an equal reverse bending moment over the Britannia pier, but although some reduction was obtained at mid-span, doubts remained as to whether he had achieved the full benefit for which he had hoped. The figures quoted by Stephenson to Capt. Simmons sounded suspiciously optimistic, for he claimed that the maximum tension stress had been brought down from 5.15 tons per square inch to 3 tons per square inch but previously there was no means of checking this. The conclusion reached from the test results was that the 102 metric ton wagons could be run over the bridge safely and without restriction, although a full train would have far exceeded the original design load. It would seem that Fairbairn had designed better than he knew, and that Clark had achieved his aims. However, this was never to be put to the test for, before this traffic could commence, the bridge was severely damaged by fire on 23 May 1970.

The Great Conflagration

After both tubes of the bridge had been completed, one of the remaining operations had been to build an overall roof for protection from salt spray which in a severe storm could blow right over the tubes. Since Stephenson was unavailable at the time, Clark was consulted. Bearing in mind the uproar that there had been over the cost of roofing the Conwy tubes with corrugated iron, he compromised by recommending an iron framework, boarded over and covered with tarred paper – presumably the forerunner of roofing felt. In due course, canvas, liberally coated with tar, was applied and so it remained until the fatal day. Fair warning that the bridge was not immune from fire was given on 13 June 1946, when at about 2.00 p.m. a painter's blowlamp set fire to timber inside the down line tube. This quickly spread to the sleepers and led to buckling of the track. All traffic was stopped for six hours, and the down line was closed for four days for repairs.

Although accounts vary somewhat in detail and various rumours were in circulation, the following statement by the former Caernarfon fire chief, F.W. Hutchinson, is probably as authoritative as any:

> The fire was caused by two schoolboys [other reports state more], who went looking for birds and bats in the upper part of the landbased tower. A hessian tarred strip which covered the recess in the land based tower (where the tube ends fitted), had worked loose, and the boys further loosened it in order to place their lighted paper to look up in to the recess for the birds. This hessian strip caught fire and within seconds the fire had travelled into the upper chamber of the tower. It was not until the fire had burned off the roof of the first landbased tower that the fire showed itself and a sightseer called the fire brigade. By that time the fire had well travelled through the apertures of the tower onto the underside of the wooden canopy covering the two metal tubes.

As misfortune would have it, a strong easterly wind carried the fire like a blowtorch through the roof void and set on fire the interior of the top cells which had been liberally painted over the years. Within half an hour the bridge was ablaze from end to end but the fire did not actually penetrate the main tubes. After fighting the conflagration for seven hours the Anglesey and Caernarfon fire brigades were forced to withdraw and leave the fire to burn itself out. An Anglesey fire officer said afterwards: 'The iron roof was red hot in places and it was like an inferno inside. We were nearly gassed and the hose nozzles were almost red hot.'

The case against the oldest of the boys involved (newspaper reports say that several boys had been dealt with earlier at a juvenile court) was heard at a special sitting of the Bangor Magistrates' Court and the proceedings were reported in the *North Wales Chronicle* of 6 August 1970. The evidence given in court differs somewhat from the Firemaster's report and accords more with other stories circulating in the area. After so many years perhaps the full story will never be known. The presiding magistrate commented adversely on the lack of security measures taken by British Railways for a vital link in communications. The seventeen-year-old defendant faced a charge of trespass, as the British Transport Police produced no evidence of malicious intent. The charge was found proven and a fine of £5 imposed.

The Phoenix Arises

An immediate effect of the fire was to cause the site joints within the towers to fail as the tubes cooled. As a result the main tubes were found to be sagging as much as 2ft at the centre, and in places the whole weight was held by only one cast-iron girder. Should this have failed, the tube would have plunged unhindered into the water. A team of experts was sent by British Railways to assess the situation and after the tubes had cooled the engineers were able to scramble on top. It was while men were on the tubes that another joint failed, but fortunately there was sufficient bearing to prevent it falling. It was clear at an early stage of the inspection that there was no prospect of saving the bridge, particularly the south tube which was the worst affected, and the most urgent task was to prevent any further collapse. No.8 Field Squadron of the Royal Engineers was called in and with the use of portable bridging components they were able to build supporting columns at each tower in the recesses in the stonework. Any immediate danger was averted.

An urgent decision on the future was essential, for the effect on the relatively fragile economy of Anglesey was disastrous. Such heavy industry as there was, consisting of the Rio Tinto Zinc Corporation, Associated Octel and the Wylfa Head nuclear power station, depended heavily on rail transport and British Railways had just made a major investment in two container ships and handling facilities at Holyhead. Within days some 300 men had been laid off by British Railways alone and local feelings were running high by July due to an apparent lack of progress. Action was demanded from Ted Heath's government. Earlier schemes for a new road crossing were put on hold until the situation could be resolved.

The design consultants were Husband & Co. of Derby, who proposed twin steel aches between the original towers. The Admiralty had long ceased to concern themselves with navigational hazards in the Strait. Initially the arches provided a working platform on which the tubes could be dismantled and a new rail deck built. Firstly the north tube, which was in far better condition, could be supported from the new arches, allowing single line rail traffic to be resumed in January 1972. At the same time, the south tube was removed and the new rail deck installed. By December 1973 the new permanent track entered service and the north tube was dismantled. Double track was not restored since automatic signalling was installed to allow the passage of twelve trains an hour on the single line. The whole reinstatement is said to have cost British Railways £3¼ million, though much of this may have been covered by insurance. Fortuitously, the rail authorities had found themselves relieved of an elderly white elephant.

There was another major bonus, supporting the old saying about it being an ill wind that blows no one any good. At the request of the Ministry of Transport, the design brief included provision for a road deck to be built above the railway and this was achieved at a cost of £400,000, whereas the urgently needed new road bridge to relieve Telford's creaking masterpiece would have cost many times as much. To make room for the road deck it was necessary to disembowel the towers, with little regard to the aesthetics of Francis Thompson's grand conception. In retrospect, without in any way disparaging a fine modern bridge, it might have been a lesser act of vandalism to have reduced the towers to deck level. Now they stand as a sad reminder of what was once one of our greatest engineering landmarks. Only the Conwy tubes remain to awaken memories of one of the supreme masterpieces of Victorian bridge-building and of the men who built it.

The old Britannia Bridge, with its slim tubes and monumental stonework, will long be mourned for it belonged to a heroic age of railway engineering which will never be seen again. So too we must hope that the age of enlightenment – that brave new world, which reduced the Euston Arch and the Great Hall to rubble and gave us New Street Station – is gone forever. The loss of Britannia was a tragic accident, but only small minds could justify the wanton destruction at Euston Square. The renaissance of St Pancras Station and its long neglected Hotel is a pointer to the way ahead in the twenty-first century when old and new can be seen to exist in harmony. Given kinder treatment than the Forth Rail Bridge has received, the new Britannia may yet celebrate its centenary.

Bibliography

Anderson, V.R., & Fox, G.K., *An historical survey of Chester to Holyhead Railway* (Oxford, 1984)

Anon, 'Centenary of the Britannia tubular bridge', *Railway Magazine* (1950), pp.331-33

Anon, *A description of the Conway and Britannia tubular bridges ... also of the Conway and Menai Suspension Bridges* (Shone: Bangor, 1849)

Anon, *The triumph of science. An account of the grand flotation of one of the monster tubes over the Menai Straits, Britannia Bridge* (Rees: Caernarvon, 1849)

Banbury, Philip, *Shipbuilders of the Thames and Medway* (David & Charles: Newton Abbot, 1971)

Baughan, Peter E., *The Chester and Holyhead Railway, Volume I: The main line to 1880* (David & Charles: Newton Abbot, 1972) [The definitive early history. The second volume was not published.]

Baughan, Peter E., 'Arches for Britannia', *Railway Magazine*, November 1970, pp.594-98

Beckett, Derrick, *Stephenson's Britain* (David & Charles: Newton Abbot, 1984)

Beazley, E., *The Menai suspension bridge 1819-26 & Britannia Bridge 1845-50* (Ancient Monuments Society: London, 1985)

Billington, David P., *The Tower and the Bridge. The new art of structural engineering* (Basic Books (Harper & Collins): New York, 1983)

Carter, Oliver F. FRIBA, 'Francis Thompson 1808-95', *Back Track*, April 1995, pp.213-18

Charlton, T.M., *A history of theory of structures in the nineteenth century*, pp.19-28 (Cambridge University Press, 1982)

Clark, Edwin, *Britannia and Conway tubular bridges* (Day & Son: London, 1850)

Clark, Latimer, *General description of the Britannia and Conway tubular bridges by a resident assistant,* (Chapman & Hall, 1849)

Conder, Francis, *Personal recollections of English engineers* (Hodder & Stoughton, 1868). Reprinted as *The men who built railways* (Thomas Telford, 1983)

Dempsey, G. Drysdale, *Tubular and other iron girder bridges* (Virtue & Co: London, 1850; reprinted in facsimile by Kingsmead Reprints: Bath, 1970)

Dunn, J N., *The Chester & Holyhead Railway* (Oakwood, 1948)

Fairbairn, Thomas, *Truths and tubes on self-supporting principles, a few words in reply to the author of 'Highways and Dryways'* (London, 1849)

Fairbairn, William, *An account of the construction of the Britannia and Conway tubular bridges and a complete history of their progress* (John Weale & Longman, Brown, Green & Longmans: London, 1849)

Gale, W.K.V., 'The rolling of iron', *Transactions of the Newcomen Society*, Vol.37 pp.35-46

Gordon, Prof. J.E., *Structures* (Pitman Publishing, 1979)

Gresham, Colin, 'The Britannia Bridge', *Transactions of the Caernarfonshire Historical Society*, 1948, pp.46-48

Gwynedd Archives Service, *Menai Bridges* (Welsh Arts Council: Cardiff, 1980)

Head, Sir Francis Bond, *Highways and dryways, or the Britannia and Conway tubular bridges* (London, 1849)

Husband, H.C. & R.W., 'Reconstruction of the Britannia Bridge, Part 1, Design: Part 2, Construction', Proc.ICE. Paper 7704. Part 1. Vol.58 February, 1975, pp 25-66

Jackson, T., *The tourist's guide to the Britannia Bridge*, 4th ed. (London, 1850)

James, John G., 'The evolution of iron bridge trusses to 1850', *Transactions of the Newcomen Society*, Vol.52, 1980/81, pp.67-101. [An extraordinarily detailed survey and a standard reference work.]

Jefferson, John C., *The life of Robert Stephenson*, two volumes (Longman, Roberts & Green: London, 1864) [The chapter on Iron Bridges was contributed by William Pole, Vol.2, pp.30-72.]

Lewis, Brian, 'Brotherton tubular bridge: a surprising miscalculation', *Journal of the Railway and Canal Historical Society*, Vol XXVIII No.6, November 1985, pp.252-361

Marshall, John, *A biographical dictionary of railway engineers* (David & Charles: Newton Abbot, 1978) [An essential reference work, new edition due.]

Millar, John, *William Heap and his company*, 1975 and later editions (published privately by Heap & Partners Ltd, Hoylake, Wirral) [A valuable history of the Canada Works, Birkenhead.]

Parry, Edward, *Parry's railway companion from Chester to Holyhead* (Chester, 1849). Reprinted facsimile E. & W. Books (Publishers) Ltd, 1970

Peters, Tom F., *Building the nineteenth century* (MIT Press: Cambridge (Mass.), 1996) pp.159-78

Petroski, Henry, *Design paradigms: Case histories of error and judgement in engineering* (Cambridge University Press (USA), 1994), pp.99-120 ('The Britannia Bridge: A paradigm of tunnel vision in design')

Pole, William, *The life of Sir Wiiliam Fairbairn, Bart* (Longmans, Green & Co., 1877, reprinted by David & Charles: Newton Abbot, 1970), pp.195-214

Pole, William, *On the strength and deflection of beams, with applications to the Britannia and Conway Bridges* (published privately: London, 1850)

Pottgeisser, Hans, *Eisenbahnbrücken aus zwei Jahrhunderten* (Birkhauser Verlag: Basel, 1985) pp.58-66 [German text. The historical importance of the bridge in Germany – Britannia Bridge occupies three per cent of the book!]

Richards, R., *Two bridges over Menai* (Gwasg Carreg Gwalch: Llanrwst, 1996)

Roberts, O. Glynne, 'The Britannia Bridge', *Transactions of the Anglesey Antiquarian Society*, 1946, pp.92-112

Rolt, L.T.C., *George and Robert Stephenson: The railway revolution* (Longmans, Green & Co., 1960)

Rosenberg, Nathan, & Vincenti, Walter G., *The Britannia bridge: The generation and diffusion of technological knowledge* (MIT Press: Cambridge (Mass), 1978)

Ryall, Dr Michael J., 'Britannia Bridge: from concept to construction', Paper 11736, Proc.ICE., *Civil Engineering*, May/Aug 1999, pp.132-43

Simmons, Capt. Lintorn A. RE, *Report to the Commissioners of Railways on the Britannia Bridge*, 18 March, 1850 [Parliamentary Papers]

Smiles, Samuel, 'Lives of the engineers George and Robert Stephenson', *The Locomotive* (John Murray London, 1904) [Various editions from 1857]

Smiles, Samuel, *Industrial Biography* (John Murray, 1882) pp.299-355

Smith, Stanley, 'The development and use of the tubular beam', *History of Technology*, Vol.14 (Mansell: London, 1992) pp.100-34

Stephenson, Robert, 'Iron Bridges', *Encyclopaedia Britannica*, 8th ed. Vol.12 (Adam & Charles Black: Edinburgh, 1856) pp.575-610

Stretton, Clement E., *History of the Britannia tubular bridge* (Leeds, 1900) [Verbatim reprint of lecture.]

Timoshenko, Stephen P., *History of strength of materials* (McGraw Hill Book Co: New York, 1953) (Reprinted by Dover Publications Inc: New York, 1983) pp.156-62

Tomlinson, Charles (Ed)., *Cyclopaedia of useful arts* (James S Virtue, c.1851) pp.242-52

Tyson, Stanley, 'Notes on the history, development and use of tubes in the construction of bridges', *Industrial Archaeology Review*, Vol.2, Part 2 (Association for Industrial Archaeology/Oxford University Press, 1978)

Walker, Charles, *Thomas Brassey, railway builder* (Muller, 1969)

Wardle, J.B., & Lucas, J.C., *Britannia Bridge. Stress investigation before and after the fire*, Proc.ICE, Part 1, 1975, Vol.58, May, pp.177-93, 673

Wilson, Paul N., 'The Britannia tubular bridge', *Industrial Archaeology*, August 1972, pp.229-41, 321-24

Chronology of the Britannia and Conwy bridges

17/03/44	Chester & Holyhead Bill.
04/07/44	Royal Assent granted.
– /08/44	Route via Britannia crossing approved by CHR.
01/03/45	First sod for railway cut.
– /03/45	First drawings for elliptical tubular bridge.
07/04/45	Captain Vidal reports.
14/04/45	J.M.Rendel reports.
16/04/45	Sir John Rennie reports.
– /04/45	Fairbairn visits Stephenson's office.
05/05/45	Chester & Holyhead Bill No.2. House of Commons Committee. Stephenson proposes tubular bridge.
30/06/45	Act receives Royal Assent.
06/07/45	First circular tube test at Millwall.
07/07/45	Second circular test.
11/07/45	Third circular test.
12/07/45	Fourth & fifth circular tests.
19/07/45	Stephenson invited to Millwall tests on 30/07/45.
21/07/45	Stephenson presses for tests on elliptical tubes.
30/07/45	Sixth, seventh & eighth circular tests.
31/07/45	Ninth circular test.
31/07/45	First, second & third rectangular tube tests.
01/08/45	Fourth & fifth rectangular tube tests.
02/08/45	Sixth rectangular tube test.
03/08/45	Seventh rectangular tube test.
04/08/45	Eighth rectangular tube test.
05/08/45	Ninth rectangular tube test.
06/08/45	First elliptical tube test.
06/08/45	Visit to Millwall by several directors and Secretary.
10/08/45	Tenth rectangular tube test.
20/08/45	Eleventh & Twelfth rectangular tube tests.
07/09/45	Second elliptical test.
18/09/45	Third, fourth & fifth elliptical tests.
19/09/45	Eaton Hodgkinson's first visit to Millwall.
20/09/45	Sixth elliptical test.
20/09/45	Thirteenth rectangular test.
20/09/45	Fairbairn suggests square or circular cells for top.
08/10/45	Tenth & eleventh circular tests.
09/10/45	Twelfth circular test.
09/10/45	Fourteenth rectangular test.
14/10/45	Fifteenth rectangular test. Two circular top cells.
09/02/46	Reports submitted to directors by Stephenson, Hodgkinson and Fairbairn.
11/02/46	CHR Board approves Thompson's drawings for piers.

(The dates 07/04/45, 14/04/45 and 16/04/45 are bracketed together with the note: "On site at Britannia Rock concerning navigation and minimum channel clearances.")

– /03/46	Hodgkinson continues experiments for Stephenson and Fairbairn continues tube development independently.
17/03/46	Contract drawings completed for piers on both sites.
10/04/46	Britannia foundation stone laid by Frank Forster.
24/04/46	Fairbairn orders model tube with cellular top.
12/05/46	Conwy foundation stone laid by Alexander M. Ross.
13/05/46	CHR Board appoints Fairbairn joint engineer for bridges with Stephenson.
– /06/46	Blair completes working drawings for tubes.
08/07/46	Tenders accepted for workshops.
14/07/46	Clark obtains idea for lifting tubes into place.
15/07/46	Fairbairn sends proposals for floating tubes to Stephenson.
29/07/46	Tenders accepted for 8,000 tons of iron.
07/08/46	G.B.Airy consulted by Clark.
11/08/46	Sites decided on for staging and workshops.
– /08/46	Decision to erect lifting presses above tubes.
– /08/46	First orders for plates sent out.
– /08/46	Stephenson goes abroad for five/six weeks.
– /09/46	British Association meeting at Southampton. Hodgkinson lays claim to concept of cellular tops.
27/09/46	Preliminary specifications for tubes posted to potential contractors.
06/10/46	Tenders for tubes due for return.
25/10/46	Stephenson claims concept of cellular bridge at Ware.
06/11/46	Final working drawings for tubes completed.
11/01/47	Sites pegged out for staging and workshops.
15/01/47	Drawings for staging and workshops completed.
– /01/47	Directors complain of rising costs of experiments by Eaton Hodgkinson.
– /02/47	William Evans starts punching plates at Conwy.
25/02/47	Clark suggests single row of top cells.
27/02/47	Hodgkinson experiments finish.
– /02/47	Staging at Menai for two tubes completed.
03/03/47	Stephenson approves single row of top cells.
24/03/47	Fairbairn completed drawings for lifting gear.
08/04/47	First rivet driven at Conwy by Clark.
24/04/47	Easton & Amos complete drawings for presses.
12/05/47	Tenders accepted for presses and lifting chains.
– /06/47	Bottom cells of first Conwy tube completed.
13/06/47	First delivery of iron to Menai.
– /07/47	Completion of staging for Menai tubes.
10/08/47	Clark drives the first rivet at Menai.
23/08/47	Stephenson confirms that Fairbairn should equally share all responsibilities on bridges.
– /11/47	Lifting chains and presses delivered from London.
03/01/48	First Conwy tube completed.
– /01/48	I.K. Brunel and Capt. Claxton visit Conwy.
24/01/48	First Conwy tube ready for deflection tests.
20/02/48	Stephenson arrives at Conwy to supervise floating.
06/03/48	First Conwy tube floated out.

11/03/48	In position ready for lifting.
16/04/48	First Conwy tube in final position.
18/04/48	Stephenson drives first locomotive over Conwy tube.
– /04/48	Capt. Simmons inspects first Conwy tube.
01/05/48	First Conwy tube opened to traffic.
16/05/48	Fairbairn advises Stephenson of intention to resign.
17/05/48	Stephenson's speech at Conwy claiming priority for conception of cellular structure at Ware.
22/05/48	Fairbairn submits formal resignation to directors.
27/07/48	Lines on Anglesey approved by Capt. Simmons.
01/08/48	Lines on Anglesey opened for public service.
12/08/48	Death of George Stephenson.
30/08/48	Stephenson's carriage run into at Conwy.
12/10/48	Second tube floated out.
– /11/48	Work in hand on Britannia land tubes.
16/12/48	Second Conwy tube ready for traffic.
02/01/49	Captain Simmons inspects second Conwy tube.
22/02/49	Shore piers completed.
– /04/49	CHR Board authorises work on Britannia second line.
04/05/49	First Britannia (Anglesey) tube completed.
20/06/49	First Britannia (Anglesey) tube floated out.
22/06/49	Britannia tower topped out by Stephenson.
10/08/49	First Anglesey tube lifting starts.
17/08/49	Hydraulic press fails. Lifting stopped.
01/10/49	New press. Lifting restarted.
06/10/49	First tube lifting completed.
10/11/49	First Anglesey tube in final position.
– /11/49	Anglesey main and shore tubes connected.
20/11/49	Anglesey hydraulic press falls in water.
End 11/49	Stephenson arrives at Menai.
04/12/49	Second (Caernarfon) tube floated out.
07/01/50	Second (Caernarfon) tube in place.
03/03/50	Caernarfon shore tube lowered and joined.
04/03/50	Tubes united continuously end to end.
05/03/50	Last rivet. First train passes through.
15/03/50	Captain Simmons inspects first completed tube.
18/03/50	Single line opened for passengers.
10/06/50	Third (Anglesey) tube floated out.
11/07/50	Third (Anglesey) tube in final position.
25/07/50	Fourth (Caernarfon) tube floated out.
31/08/50	Stephenson offered knighthood at Newcastle.
19/10/50	Capt. Simmons inspects completed Britannia.
– /08/51	Grand Banquet for Stephenson at Bangor Ferry.
13/10/52	Queen Victoria and Prince Albert cross Britannia.

Index

Page numbers in *italics* indicate illustrations.

Horton, J., 102
Howard & Ravenhill, 100
Jackson, T., 70
Kennard, T.W., 145, 147
Kennedy & Vernon, 120
Mare, C., 103
Nowell, B., 58, 63
Pearson, C., 58
Peto, Brassey & Betts, 73
Peto, Brassey, Betts & Jackson, 129
Price, E., 126-27
Roberts, R., 71-72
Thomas, J., 60
Thorneycroft, G.B., 68

Engineers

Airy, G.B., 44-45, 149
Baker, W., 147
Barton, J., 113
Barlow, W.H., 148
Berkeley, G., 36, 50
Bidder, G.P., 19, 31, 32, 49, 117
Bouch, Sir T., 148
Bow, R.H., 147-48
Brewster, Sir D., 115
Brunel, I.K., 76
Clark, E., 14, 47-49
Clark, L., 116
Claxton, Capt. C., 76, 106
Colburn, Z., 138
Cowper, E.A., 111
Cubitt, J., 145
Cubitt, Sir W., 116
Dockray, R.B., 125
Fairbairn, T., 38, 115
Fairbairn, W., early days, 13; views on
    continuity, 17; meets G. Stephenson, 18;
    meets R. Stephenson, 18; Millwall tests,
    38-40; Report to Directors, 41; model
    tube, 42-43; final design, 46; lifting gear,
    100; tubes for Menai, 102; dispute with
    Stephenson, 114-18; box girders, 119-25
Forster, F. 20, 44, 58-59
Fowler, Sir J., 85, 120-21, 124
Fox, C., 29, 55
Galbraith, W., 147
Giles, F., 25
Gooch, T., 29, 91-92, 94
Gregory, C.H., 138
Grove, G., 20
Harrison, G., 132
Harrison, T.E., 112
Hartley, J., 146
de la Haye, J., 34
Heap, W., 68, 77, 132
Hodgkinson, E., 15, 17, 37, 39-41, 73, 75,
    98-100
Inglis, Prof. C.E., 80
Lee, H., 20
Jacomb, W., 145
Keefer, T.C., 129
Latham, J.H., 141, 148

Le Fanu, W., 120
Locke, J., 92, 111
Macneill, Sir J., 17, 32, 145
Marshall, W.P., 36
May, C., 119
Moseley, H., 81, 86
Osborne, R.B., 142
Phipps, G.D., 116
Pole, W., 17, 82, 86, *87*
Rammell, T.W., 35
Reilly, C., 148
Rendel, A., 148
Rendel, J.M., 24
Rennie, J., 24
Rennie, Sir J., 24
Robertson, H., 92
Ross, A.M., 20, *65*, 66-67, 79
Russell, J. Scott, 38
Sacré, C., 123
Stephenson, G., 11, 18, 28
Stephenson, G.R., 113, 118
Stephenson, R., early days, 11; chief
    engineer LBR, 12; meets Fairbairn, 18;
    organisation, 20; chief engineer CHR,
    27; cast-iron arches for Menai, 33;
    pressure of work, 37; tube tests, 39;
    Report to Directors, 41; appoints Clark,
    48; problems at Brotherton, 50;
    approves floating of tubes, 60; first train
    over Conwy, 76; Chester inquest, 92;
    elected MP, 94; at Menai, 106, 108-09;
    box girders, 125; Egyptian bridges, 126-
    27; visits Montréal, 130
Stephenson, R. & Co., 54
Stockman, B.P., 113, 126-27, 134
Tate, G., 66, 139
Telford, W., *22*, 26
Thomson, J., 20, 32, 145
Thompson, F. (architect), 56, 61, *65*, 134
Vignoles, C.B., 16, 25, 31, 92, 109, 120
Walker, J., 26, 93
Warren, J., 145
Wennington, W.V., 119
Wild, C.H., 16, 20, 106, 126, 145

Foremen and Supervisors

Blair, 38, 46, 68, 98
Graham, J., 38
McLaren, J., 20
Murray, J. (ship designer), 38
Rolfe, C., 20, 107
Ross, H., 38

Railway Inspectors (all Royal Engineers)

Coddington, Capt. J., 53, 91
Pasley, Maj.-Gen. Sir G.W., 21, 91-93, *93*,
    109
Wynne, Capt. G., 30, 50, 53, 121
Simmons, Capt. J.L.A., 76-78, 85-86, 93,
    108, 109-10, 121-22
Tyler, Capt. Sir H.W., 122, *123*